The Tunnels Under Our Feet

COLORADO'S FORGOTTEN HOLLOW SIDEWALKS

Tracy Beach

BOWER HOUSE

DENVER

BowerHouseBooks.com

Cover Design by Margaret McCullough
Text Design and Layout by D.K. Luraas

Printed in Canada

Library of Congress Control Number: 2014941784

Contents

Introduction v

1. The Original Underground 1

2. Letting in the Light 3

3. Constructing the Historic Underground 8

4. The Choice to Preserve or Destroy the Underground 10

5. The Surprising Discovery of the Paranormal in the Underground 14

6. Tours of the Historic Underground Across the U.S. 18

7. Pueblo 25

8. Victor 41

9. The Stanley Hotel—Estes Park 50

10. Denver 53

11. Durango 70

12. Salida 82

13. Cañon City 99

14. Florence 111

15. Trinidad 124

16. Colorado Springs 131

17. The Broadmoor—Colorado Springs 139

18. Old Colorado City 143

19. Cripple Creek 149

20. Leadville 154

21. Fort Collins 159

22. Watching History Being Destroyed 167

Bibliography 171

Index 173

Contents

Introduction

Have you ever wanted to go through a trap door to see what was behind it? Have you ever wanted to walk through the basement of a musty, dark, hundred-year-old building to find a secret passage?

I have spent most of my life in the heart of the Rocky Mountains. I dig for gemstones, agate, and crystals. I climb mountains just to have the chance to investigate old ghost towns. I'm also fascinated with the tales of the red light districts and the "painted ladies" of the Old West. In 2008, my local library had just uncovered a 1940s interview with a madam, and I eagerly immersed myself in her life … and that's when I saw it.

The interview talked about tunnels underneath the streets and sidewalks. She talked of how men would use these tunnels to sneak around town to visit the "girls." My adventurous side kicked in and I was now determined to find them.

I started with the town historian, and he said they were a myth. I visited the local history museum and was told the tunnels were just stories, but as I was walking out, the secretary slid a piece of paper into my hand.

I called the woman that night and she told me about a historic building on Main Street that had a tunnel. She and her friends had sneaked into the building one night to hold a séance. They swore each other to secrecy, but she gave me the address anyway.

The next day I visited the building and asked the owner about the tunnels. He gave me a quick smile and asked me to follow him. Together we went into the building's basement and after dodging spiderwebs, he handed me a flashlight. He pointed to an old wooden door on the back wall and told me to open it. What I found on other side would consume my life for the next five years.

Do you want to know one thing I've learned from my research on Colorado's hollow sidewalks? Most people don't believe they exist … but everyone wants to know where they are.

I'd like to thank all the building owners who allowed a stranger carrying a bag of flashlights and a camera to investigate their store's basements. A special thank you to Jeffrey Donlan from the Salida Regional Library for leading me in the right direction, and a big thank you to my husband who believed in me.

If you know of any vaults or tunnels located in towns that I've missed, I would love to research them. Email me at Tunnelsunderourfeet@outlook.com

ONE

The Original Underground

Tunnels, hollow sidewalks, tombs, crypts, secret passages, vaults, sidewalk caverns, pedestrian underpasses, and catacombs. These were used to bury the dead, hold secret meetings, get from one place to another in bad weather, smuggle goods, hide illegal booze, store merchandise, hide during times of war, and as a clever way for men to sneak off to visit the local brothel.

The oldest vaults were built in Babylonia, under the Sumerian Ziggurat, in about 4,000 BCE and were built of burnt bricks with clay mortar. Egypt followed close behind and built their earliest vaults at Requagnah and Denderah around 3,500 BCE. The Etruscans, who came to central Italy from Asia Minor around 1,200 BCE, were thought to be the first to use the barrel vaulting method when constructing the vaults for their dead.

The Romans conquered the Etruscans in 264 BCE but kept a lot of their culture alive. They continued the Etruscan belief of the twelve Olympian Gods and also their architecture, such as arches, sewers, drainage systems, and barrel vaulting. The Romans are thought to be the first to use the art of barrel vaulting in large-scale projects and the first to use scaffolding.

Roman builders gradually began to design unique additions to the barrel vault and created what is now known as the groin vault and the domed ceiling. Despite being more complex to build, a groin vault did not require heavy, thick walls for support and allowed for more spacious buildings with greater openings and more light.

A groin vault, also known as a double-barreled vault or a cross vault, is produced when two barrel vaults intersect each other. A dome can be thought of as a series of arches built in a full circle around a center point, or as an altered version of a groin vault but with a raised roof.

Unfortunately, the evolution of the vault was halted around 398 CE, when Rome began to be attacked and by 476 CE, Rome fell. After the fall of Rome, vaults were not built in Rome for several centuries. Fortunately, the evolution of vault style architecture continued in other parts of the world after the fall of Rome. The Roman Empire, which dates back to 27 BCE, included countries such as Britain, Spain, Portugal, France, Italy, Greece, Turkey, Germany, Egypt, Austria, and the northern coast of Africa. While Rome struggled to rebuild, the countries it once ruled evolved the art of vault making and introduced it into their own styles of architecture. Great Britain, which was controlled by Rome from 43 CE until 410 CE, introduced vault architecture into all styles of construction, not just in the building of elaborate churches and palaces. Secret passages, crypts, vaults, and catacombs have been built all throughout the country. As the country grew, so did their need for space. Churches and graveyards were built with underground vaults to store the dead, below ground shops were built to use as much available space as possible, and secret passages were constructed to smuggle goods without paying expensive taxes. The "double cupboard," a wonderfully clever invention, was used to connect two buildings together. A secret door would be hidden inside an ordinary-looking cupboard and the exit would be through a cupboard in the adjoining building.

In the sixteenth century, as England started to colonize America, the colonists brought their knowledge of architecture with them, which included constructing underground vaults. The vault styles invented in Babylonia in 4,000 BCE would now be starting a new chapter. Surprisingly, the trip to the new world would introduce the colonists to a wonderful new invention that would change below ground vaults and tunnels forever—the deck light.

Letting in the Light

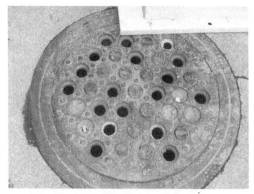

A vault light cover in Durango, originally embedded with 37 crystals that have turned purple with age and many years of exposure from the sun. It is very common to find vault covers with missing crystals due to breakage or theft.

Pavement lights, vault lights, glass bubble panels, glass sidewalk lenses, refracting lenses, and illuminating tiles. These wonderful pieces of hand-blown glass, which allowed the once-dark underground passages to be illuminated without the dangers of candles and lanterns, were realized aboard the ships that brought the colonists to America. As they sat below deck, they were able to see in the darkness thanks to the ship's deck lights.

A deck light or deck prism is a prismatic glass set into the deck of a ship to allow natural light to shine below deck. These were especially useful in areas of the ship where an open flame would be a hazard, such as a ship carrying coal or gunpowder. The deck lights also allowed a fire below deck to be discovered sooner, as it would show through the glass. Deck lights came in five prism styles: bull's eye, hex pyramid, reamer, ribbed, and rectangular. The bull's eye lenses, which are usually flat on one side and convex on the other, are thought to be the oldest style and pre-date the prismatic shapes.

A vault light cover also from Durango that originally held ten crystals. Some of the missing crystals have been replaced with concrete in an attempt to keep out the elements.

The first deck light was invented by Edward Wyndus, who patented it in 1684. By laying flat on the deck of a ship, the glass prism refracted and dispersed light into the spaces below. The small hole in the deck used to insert the deck light was small enough that it didn't weaken the planks of the ship.

Despite having the knowledge, it took one hundred and fifty years before the first patent was filed for a vault light to illuminate the below ground tunnels. The use of tunnels and vaults under the streets and sidewalks appears to have started in New York City in the early 1800s, and were illuminated by lanterns or candles.

The first vault light was invented in 1834 by Edward Rockwell. His patent was for a round iron cover, similar to a manhole cover, with a single huge glass eye in the center that was half the diameter of the iron cover. Unlike the deck lights, which were flat on the top but with a six-sided pointed prism on the bottom, his was made of flat glass that simply produced a bright spot on the floor.

In 1845, Thaddeus Hyatt filed a patent for a new and improved vault light. His version was based more on the original deck lights, but used the same iron cover designed by Rockwell eleven years

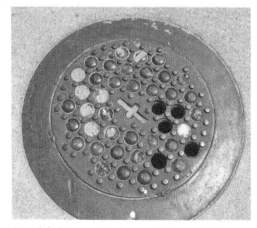

A vault light cover in Ellinwood, Kansas, that originally held forty-two crystals and has an imbedded shape in the center. This was used to lift the vault cover up in order to pour coal into the vault space below the sidewalk.

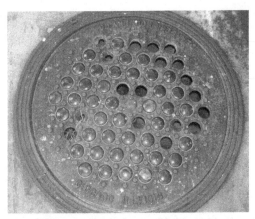

A vault light cover from Leadville that originally held sixty-one crystals.

A close-up of vault lights in Cañon City and the wonderful purple color they turned as they aged.

A vault light from Victor that was simply embedded into the sidewalk without the use of a vault light cover. These overly large crystals were placed five to six feet apart in the center of the sidewalk to allow light into the spaces below.

earlier. Instead of one large flat light, he invented an iron cover, which he called a "vault cover," and embedded it with a collection of small glass lenses set into the iron. The glass lenses were flat on the top and had a prism on the bottom. In total, Hyatt filed six patents for vault lights.

The use of vault lights continued until the 1930s, when electric lights became cheaper and produced more light for the below ground areas.

Some buildings that couldn't afford the crystal vault lights, but still wanted light to shine into their below ground spaces, used grates. The drawbacks to the grates were that they didn't keep out the weather or dirt, but did allow ventilation and light into a below ground space.

The vault light covers and grates came in many different styles, shapes, and sizes.

A manhole cover in Durango from inside a below ground vault. This shows how the vault covers were secured.

A large vault light panel in Colorado Springs. These were used to allow in a large amount of light, yet add a decorative touch to the building.

A creative use of vault lights in Denver. The combination of a vault light panel and decorative glass block adds a wonderful architectural feature to this building as well as allowing extra light into the vault space below.

A large vault light panel in Cañon City that was above an underground shop.

A large vault light panel in Trinidad from inside the below ground vault. This shows the amount of light that the vault lights produced and the wonderful prisms on the underside of the panel.

A building in Denver with large grates on each side of the front entry that are protected with a metal fence. The below ground vault area has been converted into a below ground patio area with plants and seating.

Another building in Denver, which is using a large metal grate to ventilate a below ground space. The planter is an attempt to encourage people to avoid walking on the grate.

A series of small metal grates outside a building in Old Colorado City. The owner has filled them in with concrete in an attempt to keep out the weather.

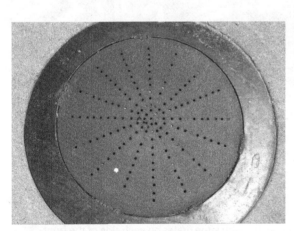

A vault light-style cover being used as a grate in Ellinwood, Kansas.

The resulting light from the grate shown at left as it shines into the vault space below the sidewalk.

A photo taken in Ellinwood, Kansas, that shows how the below ground areas were lit with oil lamps that were placed on small shelves embedded into the walls.

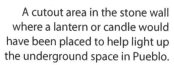

A cutout area in the stone wall where a lantern or candle would have been placed to help light up the underground space in Pueblo.

THREE

Constructing the Historic Underground

Underground hollow sidewalks and vaults had many uses when they were first installed in the late 1800s. Vaults allowed businesses to expand and utilize the unused spaces beneath sidewalks and alleys for storage and coal delivery. Hollow sidewalks allowed for delivery of merchandise, for people to travel from one place to another without being seen, and for construction of below ground shops.

A hollow sidewalk differs from a vault in that it is usually shared by all the buildings on a block and may connect many blocks together. A hollow sidewalk could also contain below ground shops with outside staircases to allow entry.

A vault and hollow sidewalk were built in a similar fashion. The underground area was normally as high as the adjacent building's basement, but a hollow sidewalk could extend beyond the sidewalk and even cross beneath the street. When these were constructed, they only needed to be strong enough to support pedestrian and horse and buggy traffic—heavy motorized vehicles were not yet invented. In areas that had trolley cars, the tunnel areas were located on either side of the tracks.

The walls of the underground areas were normally four to twelve inches thick. Some were made of brick and others were made of stone, depending on what material was readily available. The roof of the entire underground structure was usually supported by a series of steel cross beams that look exactly like railway track, and might be one in the same. A roof of concrete, wood beams, or large flat rocks were then placed over the top of the steel beams to give support to the sidewalk that would sit above it. More elaborate hollow sidewalks have arched ceilings. Historic photos show wooden sidewalks over the top of a vault space before concrete became widely used.

The main problem with the below ground areas was water damage. Water tended to find its way into the underground areas and would wreak havoc on the structural steel supports, retaining walls, and concrete encasements. Since vault covers and metal grates were used above the underground areas to allow in light and ventilation, they leaked, which added to the problem.

The steel support beams used in the construction of the below ground vaults in Durango.

The steel support beams and large stone slabs used to help support the sidewalk in Durango.

The support beams and large jacks used to stabilize a below ground vault in Durango.

An alley in Pueblo with a sinking manhole cover due to heavy delivery trucks collapsing the below ground vault.

FOUR

The Choice to Preserve or Destroy the Underground

One store owner off of Union Avenue in Pueblo took pictures of the destruction of his underground hollow sidewalk before the city filled it in with sand. The city removed the concrete sidewalk and dug out the entire hollow sidewalk, leaving just the basement side exposed. (Courtesy Pueblo City-County Library District, Western History Collection)

When someone buys a historic building and discovers it has hollow sidewalks or a vault, one of three things happen. They love the history and want to restore it or find a way to re-use it; they don't care about the history or even that it exists and just ignore it; or they see it as a hazard and an eyesore and want it removed. It could be an expensive endeavor.

In 2002, New York City spent eight weeks and $70,000 just restoring the vault lights on a fifty-four foot stretch of sidewalk. This amount did not include any restoration of the below ground vault, which luckily was still structurally intact.

In 2003, a skid steer operator in Boston was killed when a vault cover collapsed under the weight of his machine. He was clearing snow off the sidewalk during a snowstorm and wasn't aware of the below ground vault. The weight caused the bolts to fail, which pulled the angle iron away from the concrete walls of the vault. The skid steer dropped twenty feet. If the building's owner had not ignored the existence of the vault and had made sure it was structurally sound, this man would still be alive.

Unfortunately, most towns ignore the historic aspect of the hollow sidewalks and vaults and simply tear out the sidewalks, fill in the area with sand and cover it back up. Since the city normally pays for this, most store owners except this as an easy and cheap solution to their underground areas.

A close-up of the original windows that have been boarded up. In the center of the photo you can even see the missing brick where a candle or oil lamp would have been placed to allow light into the area. (Courtesy Pueblo City-County Library District, Western History Collection)

Off of F Street in Salida, a store owner was faced with the city threatening to fill in his hollow sidewalk with sand due to the collapsing sidewalk. He paid to have the sidewalk repaired and shored up his hollow sidewalk a little differently. After cleaning out all the dirt and debris, he built a structure out of two-by-fours. When I asked him why he saved his underground area, he replied, "Well, I wasn't really sure what this tunnel was used for or what I was going to do with it. But it looks like it's part of the history of the building and to be honest, it's just kinda neat."

The town of Victor decided to fill in its last remaining open hollow sidewalk, but wanted to keep a record of it. They hired a company to do an archaeological survey of the underground space before they filled it in forever. It's a shame that the town took so much time and care to record the history of the space, yet still filled it in with sand.

A close-up of the door and one window in Pueblo that will now forever be covered up with sand and forgotten. (Courtesy Pueblo City-County Library District, Western History Collection)

Owners of a historic building off of Nevada Avenue in Colorado Springs decided to save their below ground vaults, but still keep themselves safe from lawsuits. The building originally had hollow sidewalks that had already been filled in with sand by the city, but they still had huge below ground vaults that they were not going to part with. To prevent vehicles from getting onto the sidewalk areas that covered their below ground vaults, they set up railings and seating areas.

Despite not being in Colorado, Ellinwood, Kansas, is a great example of one woman's desire to preserve her building's hollow sidewalks. Owner Adrianna Dierolf documented the restoration process, which took place in the 1980s. The process was started by removing the sidewalks and exposing the underground areas. They found a collapsed outside wall, so they carefully removed the original stone and brick and set it aside to be reused. They leveled out the collapsed outside wall to allow the exterior wall to be rebuilt using the original brick and stone salvaged from the collapsed wall. The people who have chosen to restore and preserve their historic underground areas set a wonderful example of how history needs to be protected.

The structure built to shore up a hollow sidewalk in Salida.

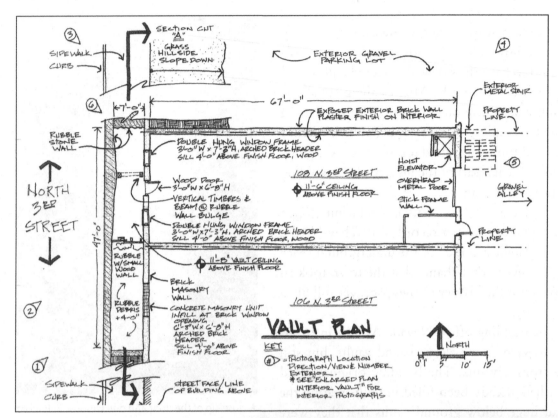

One of the drawings made to document a hollow sidewalk in Victor before the town filled it in. (Courtesy Victor Lowell Thomas Museum)

This railing and seating area has been put in place on the sidewalk to help protect the building's below ground vault. The railing helps keep vehicles from driving on the sidewalk.

The below ground vault located under the seating area in the left-hand photo. This one is being used to store the building's original cast iron radiators.

The beginning of the process as the sidewalks are removed and the underground areas exposed to repair the hollow sidewalks in Ellinwood, Kansas. (Courtesy Ellinwood Underground and Emporium)

The outside wall is leveled out to allow the exterior wall to be rebuilt. (Courtesy Ellinwood Underground and Emporium)

The exterior walls being rebuilt using the original brick and stone salvaged from the collapsed wall. (Courtesy Ellinwood Underground and Emporium)

FIVE

The Surprising Discovery of the Paranormal in the Underground

When I started doing research for this book, I quickly realized that I would have to confront one of man's greatest fears—the dark. Not really the dark, but what could be hiding in the dark. Since access to the underground is through the basements of old, historic buildings, I would have to venture into these areas armed with only a flashlight and my camera. Some basements were easy—they were clean, had swept floors, tons of lighting, and stairs that had all the steps still intact. But some basements really put me to the test—buildings that had access to the basement through a trap door hidden under a rug, no lighting, piles and piles of discarded junk, and the strong odor of mold and dirt. Luckily, I had my "team" with me, and my kids don't seem to be afraid of anything.

The first building we researched was in Salida. As I took the first series of pictures, I started to notice that strange white balls were showing up in a lot of them. I had the photos printed and did some research on them ... I had orbs.

Now, orbs are very controversial. Some people think that orbs are proof of ghosts, while others think that orbs are simply dust or bugs caught on digital cameras. I think both theories are right.

Digital cameras have a charge-coupled device (CCD) that sends out a signal that bounces off everything in its path and sends back signals—like sonar. Then the photocell decides how much light is needed for the image and the camera takes a picture of everything, including dust, bugs, water droplets ... and ghosts.

Orbs (also known as energy balls or ghost orbs) have been part of the paranormal for quite a while. Native Americans called them "Tei Pai Wankas" and believed that they were the spirits of dead relatives. In Europe they were called "Will-o-the-Wisp," and in the Old West there were stories of strange balls of light hanging around railroad tracks. About 99 percent of the orbs caught on camera are simply dust or bugs. But there is the remaining 1 percent that is actually paranormal.

First off, I'll explain what a dust orb is. In a picture that I took while beneath an old opera house, I saw a large swarm of dust orbs.

Dust orbs showing up in a photo.

They were caused from me crawling around on my hands and knees and stirring up a lot of dust, which got picked up on my camera. If you take a series of pictures of dust orbs, you will notice that they flow like a wave and have no sense of direction or purpose.

A ghost orb is defined as an orb that hovers or flies around the room, while the dust orb simply floats away. If you take a series of pictures of ghost orbs, you will notice that they actually zoom around. Ghost orbs will also drain the energy out of your flashlights and cameras. I always took a bag of batteries with me in case I came across a ghost orb. It is believed that paranormal entities need energy to manifest and they will take it from any source available. I came across a ghost orb while inside a hollow sidewalk in Salida. It had a well-defined thick white ring around it and an energy pattern inside of it.

A well-defined ghost orb.

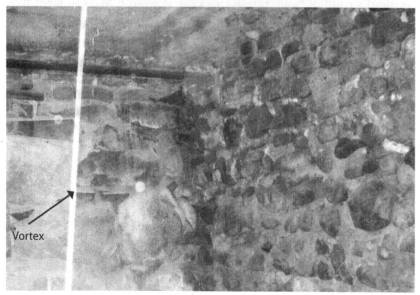

Vortex

A string of ghost orbs inside a vortex.

In another hollow sidewalk in Salida, I took a series of pictures and caught a "paranormal vortex." If you look closely, you can actually see a string of ghost orbs inside it. Paranormal researchers describe these types of vortexes as a sort of portal to the sprirt world.

While walking through a drainage canal beneath the town of Trinidad, I took numerous photos. Many residents had told us that the canal had many doors that would lead us to the underground (it doesn't). We happily took a picture of the only wood door we found in the canal, which simply was a blocked-off water overflow. When we looked at the photos, we discovered an interesting ghost orb. When I zoomed in on the ghost orb, we could see it had a face. At first we thought this was a case of matrixing, which is simply our brain's way of finding a familiar shape or image in a pattern or object—like when you see a turtle in the clouds or a holy figure in a potato chip or sandwich. After comparing it to the wood grain in the door behind it, we came to realize that it is a wonderful example of a ghost orb.

We caught a ghost orb in motion in the basement of the Elks Lodge in Victor. The photo we took shows sunlight streaking in through a crack in the window and a white streak zooming across the frame, which is the ghost orb. Despite the fact that 99 percent of orbs are dust orbs, it does make it interesting when you catch orbs on camera.

Despite the ghost orbs, my fear of the dark wore off pretty quickly as I went into dark basement after dark basement with my "teammates." The only time my son Eric got nervous was in a basement in Leadville. The area that we needed to access had been partially filled in with dirt, which caused us to have to crawl on our hands and knees to get to the front of the store where the underground would of been, but in this case, it wasn't. My son went first and held the small flashlight in his mouth as he crawled in complete darkness, with me close behind him. Halfway down he said, "There are ghosts in here!" As he continued to crawl, he mentioned them again. I reached for my camera, which was in my pants pocket, to see if we could catch them on camera. As quickly as it started, it stopped. "Sorry Mom," he said, "they were just little white mice running around."

In all the basements I've been in, I've only been bothered by one ghost. I never saw him, but I could feel him. I was down in a basement in Old Colorado City taking pictures when the room started to get real cold and the hair on the back of my neck started

My daughter in a drainage canal beneath the town of Trinidad.

A ghost orb with a face.

to stand up. As I continued taking pictures, I started to feel someone breathing down the back of my neck. I stopped, turned around, and said, "Look, I'm just taking pictures of this hollow sidewalk. I'm not hurting anything. I'll be done in a minute." Almost as quick as I turned back around, the breathing returned. I spun back around and said, " Knock it off! I'll be done in a minute!" I finished my pictures and as soon as I left that room and entered the front room, the coldness was gone and so was the creepy ghost. When I went back upstairs, I asked the store owner if she had any problems with ghosts in the basement. She told me stories of a number of ghosts in her basement and in the store itself. "But the only one that creeps me out is that guy in the basement," she said.

A ghost orb in motion—
sunlight streaking through
a crack in the window, and a
ghost orb on the left.

SIX

Tours of the Historic Underground Across the U.S.

The first question I get asked after I tell people about the historic underground is, "Where can I go see it?" Unfortunately, there are only two places in Colorado that offer tours of their underground at this time. I'm hoping that after people become educated on how important the historic underground is that more towns and cities will re-open their areas to tours. What a wonderful way to attract people to their towns during tourist season.

This chapter also covers towns and cities all over the United States that offer tours of their underground. I'm hoping that these wonderful underground museums will show Colorado what can be done to preserve our own history.

Colorado
The Stanley Hotel
333 Wonderview Avenue,
Estes Park
1-800-976-1377
1-970-577-4000

The Stanley Hotel, which opened July 4, 1909, originally became famous because it was the first fully electric hotel west of the Mississippi. It was brought back into the spotlight in 1977 when horror writer Steven King wrote the book *The Shining.*

The hotel offers many tours. One is "The Ghost and History Tour," which features the history of the hotel, including the hotel's original owner, and the story of Stephen King's historic visit. The tour also mentions ghost stories and sightings, the hotel's most famous rooms, including room #217 where Stephen King stayed, as well as the tour of the underground tunnel.

Each tour has a maximum of twenty people. No children under the age of five are allowed. No dogs are allowed on the tour. Advanced reservations are required. Tickets are $15 per person, $10 for children between the ages of five and ten. For reservations call 1-970-577-4111.

A view of the inside of the underground service tunnel at the Stanley Hotel. These tunnels were used by the staff to avoid being seen by the hotel's high-profile guests. It is believed that at one time the other buildings on the property were connected by these tunnels. No other tunnels are known to exist at this time.

The Blake Street Vault is actually not named for the wonderful tunnel entrances in the basement, but for a bank vault discovered behind a secret wall during the remodeling of the basement. The building, built in 1863, is one of the earliest brick structures in historic lower downtown Denver. The double tunnel entrances located in the basement are believed to connect to a series of hollow sidewalks that led people all around Denver, including Union Station. The doorways are five feet nine inches tall by three feet wide, but the height was originally taller—the basement floor was raised during the remodel. The tour includes a history of the building, the story of the ghost of a barmaid who sits in booth #3, a view of the bank vault that contains scratches from a man who suffocated inside, and a tour of the tunnel entrances.

Restaurant hours are Monday–Tuesday 4:00 p.m. to midnight, Wednesday 11:00 a.m. to midnight, and Thursday–Saturday 11:00 a.m. to 2:00 a.m.

Tours are free and reservations are required. Please show respect, as this is a business.

The Blake Street Vault
1526 Blake Street, Denver
1-303-825-9833

A view of the two tunnel entrances that lead into the sealed-up hollow sidewalk at Blake Street Vault.

The preserved hollow sidewalks and below ground shops of Ellinwood are a testament to one woman's love of the Old West. Adrianna Dierolf's family has owned the Ellinwood Emporium since its inception in the 1800s. Handed down from generation to generation, Adrianna was fascinated with the building and its history, but mainly with the basement. Her father had told her stories of the below ground shops and tunnels all around town—how the entire town was connected by these tunnels, the names of all the below ground shops, how the tunnels were used for tornado shelters, and how the tunnels were even used during World War 1 during the anti-German hysteria that swept through Kansas. But despite her pleading, her father would not allow her into the basement. The door was kept locked with a huge padlock. When her father lay dying in the 1970s, she sat by his bedside. But as soon as he took his last breath, she headed straight for the store and used a sledgehammer to break the old lock off the door.

Inside she found a time capsule. The tunnels, coal chutes, and below ground shops were totally intact and completely furnished. It was as if the tenants just locked the doors and walked away.

In 1982, the town built new sidewalks and was filling in all the

Kansas
The Ellinwood Emporium and
The Historic Wolf Hotel
2 and 1 North Main, respectively, Ellinwood
1-620-564-2400,
1-620-617-6915

hollow sidewalks with sand. In order to save her own building's hollow sidewalks, she invested her own money and restored them.

The buildings, which house antique shops, are open Monday through Saturday 10:00 a.m. to 4:00 p.m. and Sunday noon to 4:00 p.m. Reservations are required.

The tours, per building, are $6 for adults and children over ten, and $2 for children nine and younger. The price is $10 per adult for both tours. Tours are available on the hour.

The Historic Wolf Hotel has also been restored and rooms can be rented starting at $40 per person.

The interior of the hollow sidewalk at The Ellinwood Emporium.

Georgia
Underground Atlanta
65 Upper Alabama Street (outside the Atlanta Visitor's Center), Atlanta
1-404-523-2311 ext. 7018

During the 1920s, the city of Atlanta constructed concrete viaducts and elevated the streets one level to permit a better flow of traffic. Store owners moved their businesses to the second floor, which left the original first floors empty. In 1968, Atlanta declared the five-block area of the original downtown a historic site and it was re-opened. In 1989, the city spent $142 million restoring the area.

The fifty-minute tour will educate you on the history of Atlanta and the underground. Tours depart Thursday through Sunday at 9:30 a.m. Reservations are required.

Prices: Adults $12; Children ages six to fifteen $10; Military $10; Children five years and younger are free.

Ohio
The Ultimate Underground Tour
1218 Vine Street, Queen City, Cincinnati
questions@ americanlegacytours.com

Enjoy a stroll through the Gateway District, home to America's largest set of historical landmarks. Visit buildings that were home to over one hundred and thirty saloons, bars, beer gardens, and theaters that hosted iconic entertainers such as Charlie Chaplin and Wild Bill Hickok. Descend below the city streets to a hidden burial vault and explore newly discovered tunnels.

The tour season starts in April and is open Monday, Friday, Saturday, and Sunday. On Sundays they do not go into the crypts under St. Francis, but instead go under St. Paul's Kirche.

Tickets are $20 for adults. The two-hour tour begins at the Cincy Haus on 1218 Vine Street.

Hidden beneath the city for nearly one hundred and fifty years, Old Sacramento's underground has long been the capital's best-kept secret. Explore excavated foundations, enclosed pathways, exposed brick retaining walls, and hollow sidewalks. Above ground, your tour guide will discuss the history of the area.

The tour season starts in March and ends in November. Tickets can be purchased at the Sacramento History Museum or by calling 1-916-808-7059. Prices are $15 for adults and $10 for children aged six to seventeen. The tour is free for children under six but is not recommended.

California
Underground Tour
Sacramento History
Museum, Sacramento
1-916-808-7059

The seventy-five minute tour in Eureka Springs includes a walking tour of the area and its history. You will then be taken underground to see the original below ground storefronts and hollow sidewalks.

Price for adults is $12. Kids are free with a paying adult. Tickets are available thirty minutes before the tour starts at either the Basin Springs Park at the kiosk or at the Basin Park Hotel.

Arkansas
The Eureka
Springs Downtown
Underground Tour
Basin Spring Park Kiosk,
Eureka Springs
1-877-643-4972

The town of Havre was originally built as a railroad supply depot by the Great Northern Railroad. The buildings were made of wood and a fire quickly burned down the entire town. The town's residents moved into the basements of their stores and dug tunnels to connect the basements together. The original underground included such stores as a bank, funeral parlor, and a drug store complete with a soda fountain. When the town rebuilt, new stores were built on the ground level and the underground areas were used to house the Asian railway workers. Later, the underground was used as a bordello, speakeasy and opium den until the end of Prohibition.

The tour includes a history of the area and of the underground. The below ground rooms are filled with original antiques and completely restored. On the first Saturday in June the museum holds a history day and the underground is staged with people dressed in vintage clothes to make you feel like you are back in the Old West.

During the summer the underground is open seven days a week 9:30 a.m. to 3:30 p.m. During the winter they are open Monday through Saturday 10:30 a.m. to 2:30 p.m.

Price for adults is $12, children aged six to twelve $8, seniors sixty-five years and older $10. Children under six years old are free.

Montana
Havre Beneath
the Streets
120 Third Avenue, Havre
1-406-265-8888

Florida
Jacksonville "Top to Bottom" Walking Tour
2 West Independent Drive,
Jacksonville
1-800-733-2668

This tour is guided by a very knowledgeable tour guide who wears a jacket similar to the one worn by Andrew Jackson, whom the city is named for. The tour includes many historic buildings and the history of the city. Unfortunately, the underground portion of the tour is simply an old bank vault located in the basement of one of the buildings. After the "regular" tour, the tour guide did take my husband and I on a private tour of the real underground which included hollow sidewalks, vault lights, and underground tunnels that connected the banks together. He is hoping to include these in the regular tour as soon as they are cleaned up and restored. Please ask about them when you call to book your reservation, so you're not disappointed.

The tour is open all year, but only on Tuesdays at 10:00 a.m. The tour lasts one hour and forty-five minutes. Tickets for adults are $15 and children aged five to twelve $5. Call for reservations or purchase your tickets at the bottom of the Jacksonville Landing escalators.

A hollow sidewalk in Jacksonville, Florida, used to connect the historic banks together.

Beneath the streets of Portland, in Old Town, are the "Shanghai Tunnels." These are a network of interconnecting basements and passages that lead to the Willamette River. The story is that kidnappers would drag drugged bar patrons through these tunnels and then sell them to ship captains. The tour includes a history of the area and a tour of the tunnels and hollow sidewalks. This tour is listed as PG13 due to the subject content. The tour guide talks about dozens of topics including prostitution and murder. It's not for the faint of heart.

Prices are $20 for adults and $17 for seniors and kids aged eleven to seventeen. This tour is not recommended for children. Call for days and hours of operation.

Oregon
Portland Walking Tours
The Visitor's Center at Pioneer Courthouse Square, Portland
portlandwalkingtours.com
1-503-774-4522

The town of Pendleton was founded around 1860 and soon became known as the Entertainment Capital. Miners, cowboys, and ranchers would come to drink in its thirty-two saloons and visit one of eighteen bordellos.

The only people that weren't welcome were the Chinese. They came to help build the railroad and dreamed of opening businesses. Instead they were shunned and the town even had strict laws that the Chinese couldn't walk the streets at night. So they burrowed underground and dug tunnels from business to business and cellar to cellar. They lived and worked in the tunnels. It is estimated that between 1870 and 1930, the Chinese dug more than seventy miles of tunnels beneath the town.

The ninety-minute tour starts in the gift shop at 31 Southwest Emigrant Avenue. The tour includes a history of the area, the history of the bordellos, and then takes you into the underground. Besides the Chinese workers, the underground was used by anti-Prohibitionists and opium addicts, but also included ice cream stores, butcher shops, speakeasies, saloons, card parlors, and even a bowling alley. The tour guide tells ghost stories of the Chinese workers who stare at the tour groups as they go past and of the train robbers who died during a gun battle in the tunnels over their stolen gold. It is said that you can still hear them cry, "It's my gold!"

To continue with the Old West theme, you can stay at a restored bordello just a few steps away. The Working Girls Hotel (W.G. Hotel) is owned and operated by the Pendleton Underground Tours. The building was built in the late 1890s and was one of the town's eighteen bordellos. Rates are $75–$95 a night depending on the

Pendleton Underground
37 Southwest Emigrant Avenue, Pendleton
1-800-226-6398 (weekdays)

season and the room. No children or pets are allowed because of the large number of antiques.

The cost for the underground tour, which is open year-round, is $15 for adults and $10 for children. No children under six years of age are allowed.

Washington
Bill Speidel's
Underground Tour
Pioneer Square
608 First Avenue, Seattle
1-206-682-4646
undergroundtour.com

On June 6, 1889, at 2:39 in the afternoon, a cabinetmaker changed Seattle's history when he overturned and ignited a glue pot. The result was the Great Seattle Fire that destroyed thirty-one blocks of buildings. The city leaders decided to not only rebuild in just stone or brick, but also to raise the streets due to the problem with flooding. In order to get the streets to the newly desired level, some streets were raised twelve feet, where others were raised nearly thirty feet.

Once the buildings were re-constructed, people still continued to use the original first floor businesses, which were accessed though tunnels and hollow sidewalks. In 1907, the city condemned the underground due to the fear of bubonic plague. The underground was then used only as storage. Later it was used for illegal flophouses, gambling halls, speakeasies, opium dens, and bordellos.

The ninety-minute tour starts in a restored 1890s saloon where the history of the area is explained before going into the underground.

The tours are offered year-round. Prices are $16 for adults, $13 for seniors sixty years and older, $13 for students age thirteen to seventeen, $8 for children aged seven to twelve, and children under seven years old are free.

~

For the adventurous type, Canada, Australia, France, and the United Kingdom also offer tours of their historic undergrounds.

A great view of the underground shops and the floor joists above, which belong to the rebuilt buildings.

SEVEN

Pueblo

Is there a tunnel that leads from Union Station?

Is there a tunnel leading from the State Mental Hospital?

Is there a tunnel from the steel mill?

Are there tunnels all down Union Avenue?

Is there really a bowling alley that has a tunnel?

Surprisingly, Pueblo actually started out as four towns that merged into one back in 1894. The first town was called Fort Pueblo and was established in 1842. It was a trading center along the boundary between Mexico and the United States. A second town was established nearby in 1854 called El Pueblo. Unfortunately, both towns were attacked by Ute Indians on Christmas day and fifty-four people were massacred. Both towns were then abandoned.

In 1870, the town of Fort Pueblo had a population of 2,265 and was thriving. General William Palmer saw the need for a railroad and brought the Denver & Rio Grande Railroad into the town. Unfortunately, the railroad also wanted to establish its own town and the Pueblo Colony was established. The town was later incorporated as South Pueblo in 1873.

The railroad enabled the two Pueblos to become the "Smelting Capital of the World." The first smelter was built in 1878, and in 1879 the Colorado Coal and Steel Works built their smelter. By 1880 the two Pueblos had a population of 7,617.

In 1882, the town of Central Pueblo was established. The story goes that it was to avoid paying taxes.

Then in 1886, a town called Bessemer was established around the Bessemer Furnace to house the workers. This started to cause problems. The residents of the three other Pueblos decided that it didn't make any sense to have four towns. In 1894, the town of Bessemer along with the three Pueblos all joined and became one town simply called Pueblo.

One story that I found interesting while doing research on Pueblo was about a man named Jack Allen. He built the town's first gin mill. The reason the story caught my eye was the list of ingredients he used to make his gin.

Alcohol
Chili
Colorado tobacco
Arkansas water
Old boots
Aqua fortis (nitric acid)
Rusty bayonets
Soap weed
Cactus thorns

Word has it … "It cut like a three-cornered file as it went down."

No history on Pueblo would be complete without mentioning the flood of 1921. Heavy rains on June second and third caused a break in the Schaeffer Dam at Beaver Creek, near the town of Penrose, which is about twenty-eight miles away. The first warnings reached Pueblo at 6:00 p.m. on June third, telling residents about a huge wall of water heading down the Arkansas River and urged them to evacuate to higher ground. Instead, hundreds of people rushed to the levees to watch and many more refused to leave their homes, as it was dinnertime.

Pueblo in the late 1800s. (Courtesy Pueblo City-County Library District, Western History Collection)

As the water reached Pueblo, the force of it broke the levees and many people drowned. Fires then broke out at a lumberyard, which caused floating piles of burning lumber to float down the now flooded streets. The fires would drift past, lodge momentarily against a wooden building, and set it on fire. The fire department was helpless at stopping the fires because they couldn't make it through the flood to douse the flames. At its highest point, the flood was recorded at twelve and a half feet deep at the McCarthy block at Union and Main Streets.

While doing research, I did discover short tunnels in various buildings that were used simply to transfer steam heat from one building to another, but that's not the type of tunnels I'm looking for. Those are not included in this chapter.

The 1921 flood. (Courtesy Pueblo City-County Library District, Western History Collection)

The 1921 flood after the water receded on North Union Avenue. (Courtesy Pueblo City-County Library District, Western History Collection)

Colorado State Mental Hospital

1600 West 24th Street, Pueblo

The state insane asylum officially opened on October 23, 1879, with twelve patients. Admission required a jury trial to determine sanity. The most common causes of insanity during this time were domestic trouble, religious excitement, opium addiction, intemperance (alcoholism), heredity lunacy (intermittent insanity believed to be related to the phases of the moon), old age, and epilepsy. Many homeless patients without family or friends were also admitted.

As the number of buildings on the hospital's forty acres grew, so did the need to access them at all hours. An underground tunnel system was built in the 1930s to connect all the buildings together. In all, there are over three miles of underground tunnels on the property. The tunnels were used to transport patients from one building to another, to deliver supplies, and to hold all the utilities that service the hospital buildings. Meals were also delivered using motorized food carts. In 1999, the hospital decided to only use the tunnels for the utilities. None of the tunnels leave the hospital grounds.

A 1934 photo showing the construction of the tunnels. (Courtesy CMHIP Museum)

An employee driving a cart through the tunnels delivering supplies. (Courtesy CMHIP Museum)

Inside a finished part of the tunnel showing the hallways and utilities in 1934. (Courtesy CMHIP Museum)

Repairing a portion of the tunnels in the 1970s. (Courtesy CMHIP Museum)

Colorado Fuel and Iron was founded in 1880 by John Osgood and later purchased by the Rockefeller family in 1903. They manufacture iron, steel, and products such as wire and train rails. Unfortunately, they are also remembered for the 1913–1914 coal strike that resulted in the Ludlow Massacre.

The Ludlow Massacre was an attack by the National Guard and Colorado Fuel and Iron camp guards on a tent colony of twelve hundred striking coal miners and their families on April 20, 1914. Around twenty-five people were murdered when the company fired machine guns at the miners. Two women and eleven children also burned to death after being trapped in a crawl space under a tent.

The tunnel, used by the Colorado Fuel and Iron workers, was used to allow safe passage from the buildings on one side of the road and the steel plant on the other. When a worker entered the turnstyles he would deposit a token with his name into a box. When he left, he would retrieve his token. This allowed the company to keep a head count of their workers. In the 1950s, the tunnel had to be re-worked and extended when Interstate 25 was constructed. The tunnel was last used in the late 1990s.

Colorado Fuel and Iron Company
Pueblo Steel Workers Museum
215 Canal Street, Pueblo

The main tunnel entrance from the inside.

The main entrance into the tunnel. The turnstyles can be seen.

The inside of the tunnel with my assistant, India, standing in the center to show the size.

Pinelle's Bowlero Lanes
1000 West 6th Street, Pueblo

A view of the inside of the tunnel.

The building, which houses a very impressive bowling alley, was built in the 1940s. The tunnel system, which is still in use today, gives us a wonderful look into the past uses of tunnels. Like the historic tunnels it is patterned after, the tunnel is used and shared by all the businesses of the building. Each business has a door that leads into the shared tunnel that allows them to access storage and use of the freight elevator. The tunnel also holds all of the building's utilities and allows for easy access in case of a building issue.

The building itself has its own history. The basement, which now houses the bowling alley, was originally built as a bomb shelter during the Cold War. The bowling alley, which was built in 1959, makes use of every square inch of the original bomb shelter. It houses thirty-two bowling lanes, a snack bar that serves their famous Italian sausage sandwiches, a bar, an arcade, and a lounge.

Ghost Building
Near Santa Fe and 2nd Street, Pueblo

The photo below, taken around the late 1800s or early 1900s, shows an old brick building that has been torn down. If you look closely, you can see the remains of a tunnel in the foundation. This tunnel appears to run between the two stores and toward the street. This type of tunnel matches many of the stories I have been told from store owners in the area, who have sealed up their tunnels when remodeling their basements.

The arrow points to a tunnel in a demolished building's foundation. (Courtesy Pueblo City-County Library District, Western History Collection)

A window, complete with a windowsill, was found in the basement of the antique shop along with a bricked-in doorway. It is likely the basement was used as a below ground shop as the room has lath and plaster walls. The thin strips of wood (laths) provided a foundation for the plaster, and was used until the late 1950s. More than likely, the sidewalk area above the window had a grate that allowed light and fresh air into the basement.

Olde Time Antiques

204 South Union Avenue, Pueblo

The window with the frame still intact. On the walls the lath and plaster can still be seen.

A bricked-in arched doorway.

I was contacted by the Bureau of Public Works about a below ground vault the city had found in an alley that was causing the street to cave in. They explained that these old vaults are all over the city and they simply open them up and fill them in with sand, but they had heard that I was doing research on them and invited me to join them. They explained that this vault was at one time used by a laundry service, which was located in the building that used to stand in the now empty field. After sending in a city employee

Ghost Building

4th Street alleyway near Santa Fe, Pueblo

to check the vault for safety and toxic gases, I was suited up and lowered into the vault through a manhole using a tripod-style hoist.

Inside, the vault room appeared to be about twenty feet by twenty feet. I was surprised by the height of the ceiling, which appeared to be around ten feet tall. There were no indications that this room connected to anything but the original building, as it had no other doors or windows. The walls, which were brick, were covered with decorative stone. The original entrance into the building appeared wide enough for a double door and seemed very well built. Due to the amount of sand that filled in the doorway, it appeared that an attempt had previously been made to fill this vault in. For ventilation and light this vault would have had manhole covers with crystal insets similar to the manhole covers already in the alley.

Also in the alley I could see a sunken manhole cover, which indicated a collapsed vault, along with another opened vault that had already been filled in once before but was getting "topped off." It appears these below ground vaults were very common.

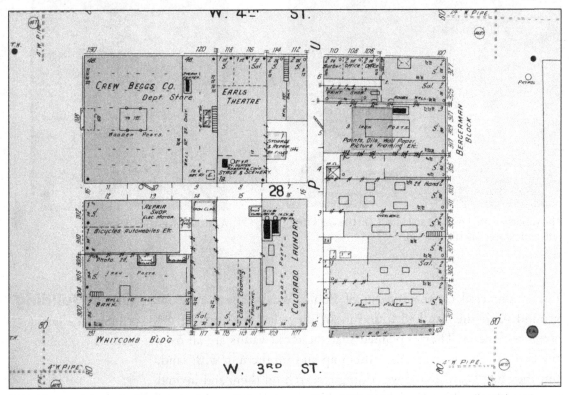

This old map of the entire block shows five vaults. I was lowered into 8/15, which was down the alley. (Photo/image provided courtesy of the City of Pueblo, Department of Public Works from historical Sanborn Fire Insurance Maps contained in the Engineering Division archives)

A picture of me all suited up and ready to be lowered into the vault. The tri-pod hoist is to my right.

The inside of the vault. The decorative stone can be seen covering part of the brick wall.

The inside of the vault showing the doorway that connected to the original building. The sand fill can be seen blocking the doorway. The toxic gas meter can be seen hanging from a rope to assure my safety.

Golden M Southwestern and Indian Art
103 West B Street, Pueblo

Doorway leading to the back entrance.

This store, which has very nice Indian and southwestern art, appears to have the only entrance into a series of five basements. Four of the basements are within the same building the store is located in and the fifth appears to be into the adjoining building.

The doorway into the basements is located outside in the back of the building. Through this doorway you enter into the basement, which has doors to the left and the right. Taking the doorway to the right, you enter into 105 West B Street. In this basement you can see a sealed-up door and window that faces the street. Continuing to the right you come to a sealed-up doorway that leads to 107 West B Street.

Back tracking into the original basement, you will see a doorway on your left that leads to 101 West B Street. This basement has a door and a window that face the back of the building. Going through yet another door you find yourself out of the original building and into the neighboring building at 327-335 South Union, which is called the Strait Block. This basement contains a sealed-up double doorway that faces the street and a bricked-in window. Despite all the basement rooms, I could find no old staircases that would allow the other stores access.

The doorway and window that faces the back of the building may have been an outside delivery door or a back entrance for a brothel, since this area was known as a red light district. The double door with a window and the single door with a window, all facing the street, would have been part of the tunnel system. Since the building faces the Union Train Station, it would be fair to say that there is a tunnel that leads from the station across the street. Denver had a similar tunnel system that allowed train passengers to access restaurants and hotels easily.

The sealed-up door and window in 105 B Street.

The sealed-up door, seen from 105 B Street, that leads into 107 B Street.

A doorway, where the door has been removed, coming from 103 B Street into 101 B Street.

The doorway facing the back of the building in 101 B Street.

The window facing the back of the building in 101 B Street.

The door leading into the Strait block building from 101 B Street.

The filled-in double door and window facing the street in the Strait block building.

The window in the basement.

Union Antiques

200 South Union Avenue, Pueblo

This store has one large window in the basement area of the store hidden behind a fence and a curtain. This window appears to be quite large and some of the original frame is still intact. A grate would have been above this window on the sidewalk to allow in fresh air and light.

I really enjoyed the owner of this store. When my daughter and I came into his store to ask about tunnels, he became very excited. He said he had a door and a window in his basement that nobody wanted to see and nobody would tell him the history of. He quickly locked the front door to his store, put the "Back in 5 minutes" sign up, and took us downstairs to proudly show us his find. And it was an amazing find! The original door and window were intact with glass panes still visible. The door has a transom window, which I have not seen before or since in any other basements.

The Edge—Ski, Paddle, and Pack
107 North Union Avenue, Pueblo

Wooden door with a transom window and original glass panels.

Large window complete with intact wooden frame and windowsill.

Johnco's Used Furniture

416 North Santa Fe Avenue, Pueblo

This basement area does not have tunnel access, but instead has a coal chute and what appears to be a below ground vault with a window in it. The sidewalk can be seen as the ceiling inside the vault and the coal chute. It appears that the floors have been raised throughout the basement, including these two areas. My assistants are posing inside the vault to show the current height.

The old coal chute.

My assistants inside the vault. The sidewalk is above their heads.

This store, which also doesn't connect to the tunnels, has two wonderful below ground vaults. It appears that it had two wide entryways that each led to a separate vault. One entryway was changed so a door could be installed. It's a shame these very nice, useful vaults have been left unused and full of rocks and dirt.

Racine's Locksmithing & Security

408 North Santa Fe Avenue, Pueblo

The sealed-up doorway to the first vault.

The second vault.

The Great Divide Ski, Bike and Hike

400 North Santa Fe Avenue, Pueblo

I have left my crown jewel for last. This store has the only historic open tunnel in the entire city of Pueblo. The tunnel itself is ninety-six feet long, ten feet wide, and has a ceiling height of eight feet ten inches. The ceiling is not flat, but instead it is beautifully arched. The size of this tunnel matches the large tunnels in Denver, which were believed to have been used to transport people or merchandise under the streets by horse and carriage. This tunnel includes a coal room and framed windows and doors.

To the opposite side of the basement are three beautifully restored storage rooms with all the original doors and hardware. One room is even listed as an explosives storage room, which shows its past life as a hardware store.

Unfortunately, the owner has informed me that the city has future plans to fill in and destroy this tunnel to make the road a few inches wider. I'm hoping that by educating people about these wonderful treasures that we can save them. I have contacted the History Museum regarding this matter.

The inside of the tunnel showing the wonderful arched ceiling and the amazing size. My assistants pose to show the height.

An original framed window complete with the original glass panels. Above the window you can see the opening where the sidewalk grate would have been to allow in light and fresh air.

The hallway which holds the three storage rooms. This one used to hold explosives.

EIGHT

Victor

Are there really tunnels under the streets?

Did the Elks Lodge really run a speakeasy?

Did the banks use the tunnels to transport gold?

Did Victor have below ground shops?

In the fall of 1891, a small mining town called Lawrence was founded. It was built to serve the prospectors in the Squaw and Battle Mountain areas. In 1893, the town was bought by the Woods brothers from J.R. McKinnie for $1,000. By 1896, the town, re-named Victor, was known as the "City of Mines." The town was named after an old homesteader named Victor C. Adams.

Victor in the late 1800s. (Courtesy Victor Lowell Thomas Museum)

With the mines demanding so much power, the Woods brothers built the first hydroelectric dam in the county of Skagway. The dam was about eleven miles from Victor and allowed Victor to become the first town west of the Mississippi to have electricity.

The below ground tunnels originally connected all the stores and hotels, on or near Main Street, with the banks. This allowed the store owners to transport their gold to the banks without being robbed. There are also numerous mine tunnels that run under the town, but it is not known if any of those connected to the underground tunnel system used by the store owners. Some mine tunnels are rumored to have connected to businesses, such as the Victor Hotel to the Gold Coin Mine, but it is not known if they connected to the underground tunnel system itself.

The Claim Jumper
106 North 3rd Street, Victor

This building, which used to be the J.C. Penny's, was built in 1899. It now houses a snack shop and the town's post office. In 2010, an archaeological survey was done on the underground tunnel in front of the building. After the survey was complete, the tunnel was unfortunately sealed up and filled in with sand.

Inside the building you can see a bricked-in window and a large bricked-in area the size of a double door. This larger area does not match the pictures taken inside the tunnel or on the drawings and its origin is questionable. The smaller bricked-in area is the window that can also be seen inside the vault.

It is also obvious that the tunnel extended farther down the street, as the end of the tunnel is simply blocked with a piece of wood.

The sealed-up window seen from inside the vault. (Courtesy Victor Lowell Thomas Museum)

The sealed-up window seen from inside the building. The large bricked-in area can be seen on the left. (Courtesy Victor Lowell Thomas Museum)

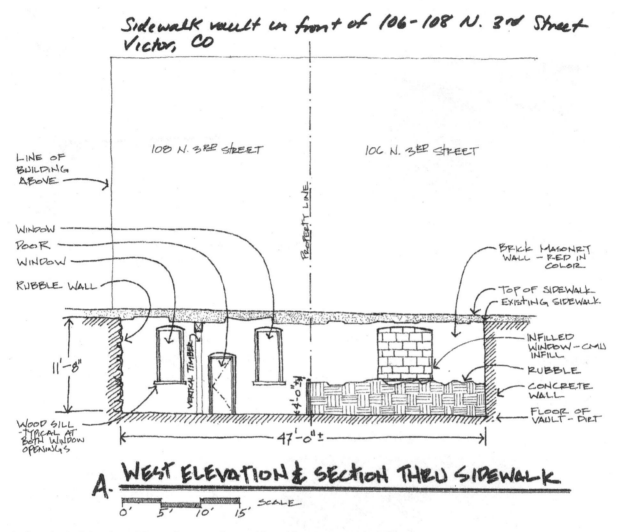

Sidewalk vault in front of 106-108 N. 3rd Street Victor, CO

108 N. 3RD STREET

106 N. 3RD STREET

PROPERTY LINE

LINE OF BUILDING ABOVE

WINDOW
DOOR
WINDOW
RUBBLE WALL

BRICK MASONRY WALL — RED IN COLOR

TOP OF SIDEWALK
EXISTING SIDEWALK

INFILLED WINDOW — CMU INFILL

RUBBLE

CONCRETE WALL

FLOOR OF VAULT — DIRT

VERTICAL TIMBER

11'-8"

4'-0"±

WOOD SILL — TYPICAL AT BOTH WINDOW OPENINGS

47'-0"±

A. WEST ELEVATION & SECTION THRU SIDEWALK

0'   5'   10'   15'   SCALE

Archaeological drawing of the underground tunnel for addresses 106 and 108 North 3rd Street.

This building is included in the archaeological survey done on the underground tunnel. The drawing above shows that this building had a door and two windows that led into the underground tunnels. From the pictures, we can see that the original wooden sidewalk is still intact and the modern concrete sidewalk was simply placed on top. Also from the pictures, we can see that the tunnel originally extended farther down the street. The stones that are sealing up the tunnel at the end are simply dry stacked—not mortared in.

Empty Building
108 North 3rd Street, Victor

The inside of the tunnel. The ladder is modern and was used to enter the area. The original wooden sidewalk can be seen, as well as one of the windows. (Courtesy Victor Lowell Thomas Museum)

One of the windows inside the tunnel, as well as an old cardboard box in the window advertising Ivory Soap. (Courtesy Victor Lowell Thomas Museum)

Kinnikinnik Emporium

318 Victor Avenue and 4th Street, Victor

This building is part of the Tatlow Block and was built in 1899. It now houses a shop that sells antiques and housewares. This building has many windows and one door that connected to the underground tunnels. A second door leads to an outside stairway, which indicates that this basement may have been used as a below ground shop.

A sealed-up doorway that leads to the underground tunnels.

A boarded-up window with the original frame.

A doorway that leads to an outside open stairway.

An outside view of the same doorway. The window can also be seen.

The Victor Elks Club was formed in 1897 and it rented or owned many different buildings before they bought their current building in 1912. This building was built in 1904 by the Colorado State Militia and originally was used as an armory.

The basement holds numerous windows and a large double door that connected to the underground tunnel system. There is also an intact speakeasy in the basement that was used during Prohibition. A speakeasy was an illegal bar that had a secret entrance accessed by telling the doorman a password. A secret set of stairs, hidden inside a false closet, allowed entry.

The original bar and liquor storage shelves are still intact. The barstools shown in the picture are not original. A large wooden door, which leads to the outside, can be seen in the speakeasy behind the bar. It is not known if this door was used for an easy exit in case the speakeasy was raided or if it was original to the basement before Prohibition.

Victor Elks Lodge
3rd Street and Diamond, Victor

The large wooden double door that led into the underground tunnels.

A sealed-up window.

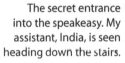

The secret entrance into the speakeasy. My assistant, India, is seen heading down the stairs.

The staircase into the speakeasy. The secret doorway can be seen at the top of the stairs.

The inside of the speakeasy. The barstools are not original.

Monarch Saloon
3rd Street and Victor
Avenue, Victor

The Monarch Saloon was built in 1899 and was also a gambling hall and a gentlemen's club. It has sat empty for many years now, and I was unable to get inside.

The outside entrance into a below ground shop.

A close-up of the door leading into the below ground shop.

The City Hall, which was built in 1900, has an interesting below ground entrance. Past the door, a sealed-up doorway can be seen. Stories of the tunnel system mention how some tunnels came down from the mines and connected to businesses or perhaps to the tunnel system itself. Could this doorway be an entrance used by a mining company so they could enter City Hall unnoticed? We may never know.

City Hall
500 Victor Avenue,
Victor

Below ground entrance into City Hall.

NINE

The Stanley Hotel

Is there really a tunnel under the hotel?

Is this where Steven King wrote *The Shining*?

Is the hotel really haunted?

Does a ghost really unpack your bags in room 217?

The Stanley Hotel was built in 1909 by Freeland Oscar Stanley and his wife, Flora. Originally from Massachusetts, Stanley was diagnosed with his second bout of tuberculosis in 1903 and was given six months to live. His three younger brothers and his mother had all died from the disease. Within seventy-two hours of getting his diagnosis, he followed doctor's orders and was on a train heading to Denver, Colorado.

When he wasn't seeing any improvements to his health in Denver, his doctor recommended spending the summer in Estes Park.

The Stanley Hotel.

Within just a few months, Stanley gained twenty-nine pounds and was able to hike five miles a day. The Stanley's bought 8.2 acres of land and built a 5,240 square foot "cottage" about half a mile west of where the hotel now stands.

Construction on the hotel began in 1907. It took three hundred men two years to build it using only hand tools. The hotel opened July 4, 1909. Stanley also built a hydroelectric plant at Fall River to furnish the hotel and the town of Estes Park with electricity. It was the first hotel west of the Mississippi to be fully electrified.

On June 25, 1911, Stanley asked for all the gas lanterns to be lit because a storm had knocked out the electricity. As Elizabeth Wilson, the chief chambermaid, walked toward room 217 with a lit candle … the room exploded. She had no idea the room had a gas leak, as no odors were added to gas back then. She was blown through the floor and landed in the dining room below, fracturing both ankles. Stanley blamed himself and paid all her hospital bills and gave her a job for life. She worked until she was ninety years old and died of natural causes. To this day, guests who stay in room 217 might have their bags unpacked or re-packed if she doesn't like you.

Despite popular belief, Steven King did not write his famous book *The Shining* in the hotel, but he did base it on his visit there.

In September of 1974, Steven King and his wife, Tabby, spent the night in the hotel. It was the last day the hotel would be open that year, as it would be closing for the winter the next day. They were the only guests in the hotel and Mr. King had a chance to tour every floor. As he walked around the fourth floor, he saw children playing ball in the hallway. He thought nothing of it, but did mention it to the bartender later that night.

The bartender tells Mr. King the history of the hotel and that those were ghost children. A little shaken, Mr. King goes to his room and that night has a terrible nightmare. He dreams that his three-year-old son is running down the hallways, looking over his shoulder screaming and being chased by a fire hose. He jumps out of bed, sits in a chair, and smokes a cigarette to calm down. He soon had the storyline for his book.

The story of the hotel's tunnels dates back to a time when servants were to keep out of sight until needed. The only tunnel that has been located is in the main building and it connects to what is now an employee lounge. It is believed that many more tunnels existed to connect all the buildings together, but no more have been found.

The door to room 217. Could that orb in the center of the door be Ms. Wilson?

The tunnel leading to the employee lounge.

TEN

Denver

Does Denver have tunnels?

Did people travel the tunnels in horse and buggy?

Did the tunnels hide the Chinese workers?

Is there a tunnel to Union Station?

Did men use the tunnels to visit prostitutes?

Did the tunnels have cable-driven carriages for the rich?

The city of Denver has had many names along with a colorful past full of lies and deception. The area was founded in the spring of 1858, after gold was discovered, and was named Montana City. By September, some of the miners decided to form a second town nearby that they called Saint Charles. Soon after, some of the miners realized that the winters were too cold and went back East. They decided to leave two men in charge to guard their new town until they returned in the spring. The first man was William McGaa, a mountain man, who was busy building his cabin. The second man was Charles Nichols, who was also building his own cabin. On November 1, 1858, miners from Montana City moved into Saint Charles and re-named it Auraria, after a town in Georgia.

On November 16, 1858, a man named William H. Larimer Jr., a land speculator, arrived in the newly named town of Auraria. He quickly sent his armed men to scout out a cabin for him and settled on the cabin that Charles Nichols was building. Larimer told Nichols that he was stealing his cabin from him and if he objected "a rope and a noose would be used on him." The local miners alerted William McGaa, who quickly came to defuse the situation. He offered Larimer and his men whiskey and in turn McGaa was given town lots and the promise that a future street would be named after him. It is unknown if Nichols got to keep the cabin.

To secure his claim on the area, Larimer officially organized the Denver City Town Company on November 22, 1858. Since the area was part of the Kansas Territory, he decided to name his one square mile town after James W. Denver, who he believed was still governor of the Territory of Kansas. Unbeknownst to him, Governor Denver had resigned just a few weeks earlier. He was reappointed to the Commissioner of Indian Affairs on November 8, 1858.

Larimer and his men spent the winter naming all the new streets after themselves—Bassett, Wynkoop, Blake, Larimer, Lawerence, Curtis, Welton, and to keep his promise, a street was also named McGaa.

In the spring of 1859, the town of Denver only had a few hundred people and only a few thousand dollars in gold dust had been found. A newspaper reporter named William Byers, who had never visited Denver, began to write fake testimonials describing Denver as "surrounded by rich gold mines." Because of the fake stories, over forty thousand people swarmed to Denver by April 1859. Unfortunately, when the miners arrived they found gold scarce and prices for supplies very high. Realizing they had been lied to, the miners threatened to burn down the town. The town was saved only by the discovery of gold in the Cripple Creek and Victor area.

The tunnels under the streets were used by many people, including the Chinese, who were possibly the reason the tunnels were built in the first place.

In the late 1870s, Irish immigrants, who were scared that cheap Chinese labor would "threaten the white working class," led a campaign to ban Chinese immigration. By 1880, the anti-Chinese movement had reached Denver, which had 238 Chinese residents. On October 31, 1880, two drunk white men began harassing two Chinese men and when the two men fled the building, the white men took chase. Soon a crowd of three thousand men, mostly Irish laborers, began to attack Chinatown and burned it down.

Despite the violence, many of the Chinese stayed and rebuilt. It is then, many people feel, that the tunnels were constructed. Like the Chinese tunnels found in many other states, they would have been used for safety and to allow the Chinese to continue doing the laundry, cooking, and housekeeping without being harassed. The tunnels were also thought to be used in the winter months to avoid the weather and for women to avoid the mud and "horse droppings" that were on the roads that could ruin their long dresses and cloaks. The tunnels would later come in handy during Prohibition.

In a 1940s interview with Laura Evens, a famous madam who owned a brothel in Denver in the late 1800s, she described the tunnels. She talked of how she entered the tunnels through a basement on Blake Street and was able to walk through Chinatown. She also mentioned how the prostitutes would take men down in the tunnels and rob them.

While doing research on Denver I came across a comical and unusual story that begs to be mentioned—"The Gravity and Bronco Street Railroad."

From 1892 until 1910, conductor John Bogue ran a horse-drawn, four-wheeled railcar. It ran from the foot of the hill on South Broadway in Englewood to the top at Cherrelyn Village. He charged a nickel a ride. A horse, which wore a straw hat, pulled the railcar to the top of the hill. Upon reaching the top, the horse named Quickstep would be unhitched and allowed to climb up the steps onto the rear platform. The railcar was then given a push by the conductor and the horse rode the car back down.

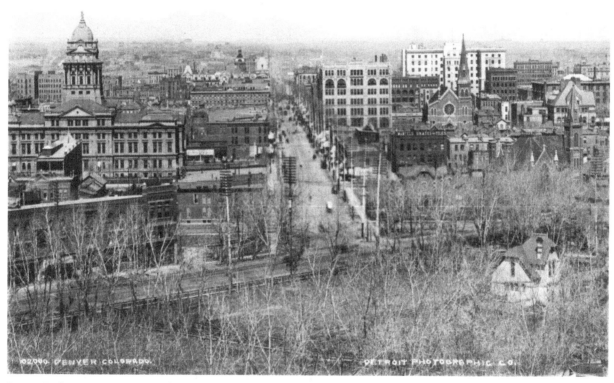

Denver in the 1890s. (Courtesy Colorado Historical Society, all rights reserved)

The Gravity and Bronco Street Railroad. (Courtesy Old Colorado City Historical Society)

Mattie's House of Mirrors

1946 Market Street, Denver

This historic building, which was built in 1889, has had many lives. Its most famous life was as a parlor house run by a madam named Jennie Rogers. After her death in 1909, the building was purchased by her rival, Mattie Silks, who ran the brothel until the city closed her down in 1915.

As a brothel, the first floor was a restaurant with a "viewing room," while the second floor housed the girls. Prices ranged from seventy-five cents up to two dollars. After the brothel closed, the building became a Buddhist temple, then a warehouse, a barbershop, a bike shop, and finally was restored into the restaurant it is today. The restaurant has pictures to honor the history of the brothel.

Inside the basement I discovered an oddly shaped hidden staircase that led up to the first floor and a sealed-up door that originally led into the underground tunnels. If only these walls could talk.

A staircase that leads to the first floor.

The sealed-up doorway that led into the tunnels.

The original tile work for Mattie Silks that is still displayed in front of the restaurant.

Rio Grande Mexican Resturant

1525 Blake Street, Denver

This building houses a very good Mexican restaurant and a wonderful door in the basement that leads to the tunnels. The basement itself was a little creepy. The owner informed me that it was, at one time, a butcher shop and showed me the original meat hooks still hanging from the ceiling. The floor had been raised way too much, which caused us to have to walk bent over in most of the basement, dodging the old meat hooks. When the owner opened the tunnel door for me, dirt spilled out and it was very obvious that the tunnel itself had been filled in. He had been told that at one time the basement area had also been used as a Chinese laundry.

The open door leading into the dirt-filled tunnel.

The Blake Street Vault

1526 Blake Street, Denver
1-303-825-9833 (call for free tunnel tours)

The building was built in 1863 and served as one of Denver's first saloons. Because of this, it also has many interesting stories. The building houses an old bank vault and an open entrance into the tunnels.

The tunnel entrances, of which there are two, are very different from the usual wooden doors I normally find. The doorways are five feet nine inches high, but the owner does admit the floors have been raised. The inside of the tunnel entrances are arched from floor to ceiling and lined with brick.

The owner gives free tours. If you go, don't forget to ask about the ghost that haunts booth number 3.

My assistants posing inside the tunnel entrance.

The inside of the tunnel entrance showing the arch of the walls and the beam helping to support the ceiling.

Both tunnel entrances. Each are seven feet deep.

Location Withheld
Downtown Denver

Not every building owner wants their address known. This restaurant owner described her tunnel entrance as "A weird little room under the sidewalk," which she then filled with garbage. In her tunnel entrance you can see a sealed-up doorway that leads straight under the street and the sidewalk can be seen directly over head. Behind the furnace I could see the rock-filled doorway that would have led down the street.

The garbage-filled entrance of the tunnel. The sidewalk can be seen above and the sealed-up door can be seen behind.

Stone-fill doorway

The inside of the tunnel. Behind the furnace you can see the stone-filled doorway.

Inside the tunnel—you can see the vault lights and the sidewalk above.

The vault lights as seen from the sidewalk.

This business has a great example of an open tunnel. This is a much better use of the tunnels than to simply fill them with sand. If you look at the very back of the open tunnel, you can see the covered-up arched doorway, behind the gray plaster, that would have allowed the tunnel to continue down the street.

EVOO Marketplace
1338 15th Street, Denver

A close-up of the windows and the stone in the open tunnel.

Arched doorway

A view of the open tunnel from the street.

Union Station

17th and Wynkoop, Denver

The entire area around Union Station is a mystery. When I spoke to the current employees, they only knew of three tunnels—a passenger tunnel, a mail tunnel, and a U.P.S. tunnel. They told me how the mail and U.P.S. tunnels were filled in with rocks and gravel back in the 1950s because they were collapsing and the passenger tunnel was filled in during the 2013 remodel. But were these tunnels the only ones filled in?

In a book titled *Denver's Railroads,* I found my answer. The authors, Kenton Forrest and Charles Albi, discuss the tunnels they discovered that connected the Elks Hotel (now the Barth Hotel), the Oxford Hotel, the Barclay Hotel, the Tramway Power House, the Windsor Stables, and the Windsor Hotel to tunnels that ran to Union Station. In a stroke of luck, a sign painter from the Tabor Hotel had taken a picture of the tunnel before the Windsor Hotel was destroyed in 1959. The tunnel appears to be quite large and could have easily held a horse and buggy or a cable-drawn carriage.

During an interview, Kenton Forrest informed me that when the book originally came out in 1981, he met a man who told him a fascinating story. The man talked of how his grandpa was a stone mason and had helped build all the tunnels to Union Station. He also mentioned how the tunnels were all under the sidewalks, but the ones at the intersections had been filled in with rocks and sand back in the 1950s, because the roads were sagging from heavy vehicles.

By following Mr. Forrest's clues, I researched all six buildings that he listed in his book as being connected to the Union Station tunnels. Mr. Forrest also supplied me with two pictures he took himself of the old tunnel entrances in the basement of Union Station.

A staircase leading into Union Station from the basement level. The tunnel doorway can be seen on the right. (Courtesy Kenton Forrest)

The Union Station entrances that lead from the tunnels. (Courtesy Kenton Forrest)

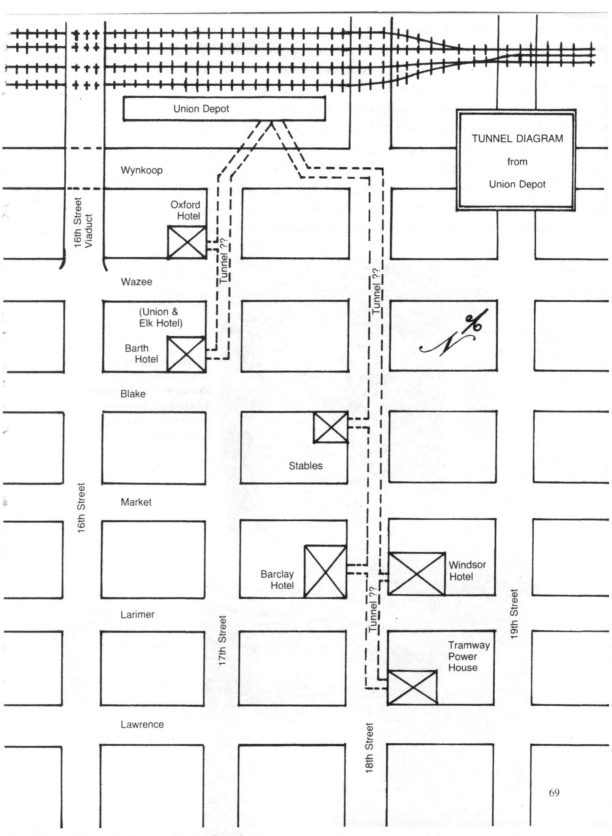

TUNNEL DIAGRAM
from
Union Depot

Union Depot

Wynkoop

16th Street Viaduct

Oxford Hotel

Tunnel ??

Tunnel ??

Wazee

(Union & Elk Hotel)

Barth Hotel

Blake

N%

16th Street

Stables

Market

17th Street

Barclay Hotel

Windsor Hotel

19th Street

Larimer

Tunnel ??

Tramway Power House

Lawrence

18th Street

69

Map of Denver's tunnels. (Courtesy Kenton Forest)

The Tramway Power House was opened in 1889 to house the power and maintenance facilities for Denver's cable car system. Could this building have powered a small streetcar that would have taken Denver's elite to Union Station through the tunnels? In London, there were tunnels designed for the use of carriages that were drawn by cables from either end. Could Denver have done the same thing? I was unable to get into the basement and was told it had been remodeled.

The Tramway Power House
1215 18th Street, Denver

Denver's first luxury hotel was opened in 1880 and torn down in 1959. The story goes that the hotel had three tunnels: one that led to Union Station, one to a horse barn, and one that led to a spa across the street. In 1959, a sign painter who worked at the Tabor Hotel took a picture of the tunnel that led to Union Station. Upon measuring the blocks in the picture, the wall appears to be ten feet high and the floor about ten feet wide. This would have allowed plenty of room for a small cable car system or a horse and buggy to take the guests of the hotel to Union Station.

The Windsor Hotel
18th Street and Larimer, Denver

The inside of the tunnel. (Courtesy Kenton Forrest)

The Barclay Hotel
18th Street and Larimer,
Denver

This building was used as an office and hotel. It was built in 1883 and torn down in 1970.

The Windsor Stables
1732–1772 Blake Street,
Denver

This building was built in 1881. The back of the building housed stables and a livery business. Is it possible that the horses were used to pull carriages to Union Station via the tunnels? I was unable to get into the building and was told the basement had been remodeled.

**The Elks Hotel
(now the Barth Hotel)**
1514 17th Street, Denver

This 1882 building originally was a warehouse. It was converted to the Union Hotel in the late 1880s, renamed the Elk Hotel in 1905, and in 1930 renamed the Barth Hotel. I was lucky enough to get into the basement and found a sealed-up door that faced 17th Street. I was told that the door originally led to a large open vault area underneath the sidewalk, which they filled in with dirt before sealing up the doorway. This would have lined up perfectly with the tunnels to Union Station.

A sealed-up doorway in the Elks Hotel that faced 17th Street.

The Oxford Hotel opened on October 3, 1891, and was Denver's first luxury hotel. In 1910, due to its intense popularity, a second building was built next door to house more rooms for the hotel. Due to many, many remodels over the years, the hotel was finally closed down in 1979 for a complete remodel to restore it to its former elegance. During the restoration, which took four years, many hidden surprises were discovered. The painted chandeliers were stripped of their paint and were found to be sterling silver. A secret boardroom was found, which contained a speakeasy used during Prohibition, and a secret entrance into the hotel's brothel was found inside a closet.

The hotel does not hide the fact that it had tunnels to Union Station and at one time used to give tours of them. In 1987, a spa was built in the basement of the 1910 building and the former tunnels to Union Station were exposed. Instead of filling them in with sand, they restored them and opened them up to allow light into the basement spa area. Inside of the restored areas you can see the sidewalk above your head and the sealed-up doorways that used to allow the tunnel to continue both to Union Station and downtown. The size of these tunnels closely matches the tunnel under the Windsor Hotel and shows that they could have been used with horse and buggy or small cable cars. An employee informed me that the hotel may resume giving tours in the future.

The Oxford Hotel
1600 17th Street, Denver

My assistant Eric standing in the tunnel entrance inside the main Oxford building. The floor has been raised.

The exposed tunnel surrounded by railings outside the 1910 building.

The tunnel facing Union Station. A bricked-in doorway can be seen.

The tunnel facing downtown. The sidewalk can be seen above and a bricked-in doorway can be seen in the back.

ELEVEN

Durango

Does Durango have tunnels?

Were the tunnels used to visit prostitutes?

Why was it good luck to sleep with a black prostitute?

Does Durango have any below ground shops?

Sometimes one bad decision can change everything. Because of one decision, the town of Durango was born and another town died.

The first town in the area was founded in August of 1876 and was named Animas City after the nearby Animas River. The name is Spanish for "the river of lost souls." By 1879, they had two hundred and eighty-six residents and attracted the attention of the Denver & Rio Grande Railroad. The track would allow silver to be brought from Silverton and would make Animas City a thriving trade center and possible location for the county seat.

The only problem was that the railroad wanted the town to give it the land for the depot, purchase company stock, and help with grading around the area. The town said no.

After the refusal, the railway chose an alternate site two miles south of Animas City. On April 14, 1880, William Bell of the Denver & Rio Grande Railroad purchased one hundred sixty acres of land for five hundred dollars and the new town was named Durango. Alexander Hunt, a former territorial governor, named the town after Durango, Mexico, where he had just traveled on business. The word "Durango" has many meanings: "meeting of the ways," "enduring," "water town," or "waterville." Other names that were considered were Smelter City and Palmer City. William Palmer was a friend and business associate of William Bell and founded the city of Colorado Springs.

In October 1880, construction was started on the Silverton smelter in the new town of Durango and was opened in August

1882. This was also the same time the Denver & Rio Grande tracks reached the town of Silverton. By 1887, Durango had smelted over a million tons of silver, lead, gold, and copper and Animas City became just a railroad stop on the line.

The town of Animas City opened up a smelter in 1885 for copper, but it failed after just a couple of years. Soon after, businesses started to move into Durango and in 1948, Animas City became part of Durango.

There are some interesting legends surrounding Durango. In the 1800s a gambling hall called "The Horseshoe" had a cage of monkeys as entertainment. When one of the monkeys died of pneumonia, the whole town mourned.

It is said that Durango wanted to be "the most musical town in southern Colorado." When the first piano came to town, it accidentally rolled down a mountainside without breaking a single string, before safely reaching its destination.

A "Negro" parlor house called "The Hanging Gardens of Babylon" had quite a business scheme to attract customers. They had the townspeople convinced that if a miner visited one of the girls that it would turn around a streak of bad luck.

Oxen pulling a building into Durango from Animas City circa 1885. (Courtesy Denver Public Library Western History Collection, #X-17762)

Old Durango circa 1920. (Courtesy Denver Public Library Western History Collection, #GB5041)

One saying I found interesting involves the words used to describe a hanging. The town people called it "Being jerked to Jesus."

When it comes to the tunnels in Durango, I'm sure some were used to visit the brothels, even though prostitution wasn't very secret. It has been said that every Saturday the parlor houses would dress up all their girls and parade them down Main Street. This was also done to advertise any new girls that had just come to town.

Some of the below ground shops in Durango are still being used and the manhole covers, with their crystals, are still found on the sidewalks around town.

Unfortunately, many of the stores that have tunnel entrances, vaults, and below ground shops did not want their names mentioned. It seems that a number of years ago a local magazine published a story about a tunnel that is still open on Main Avenue. After the article came out, the store was robbed twice using the tunnel. Out of respect, this tunnel, despite being one of only two open tunnels I found in Durango, will not be mentioned. The other is in the Strater Hotel, which I was not allowed to photograph. Of all the below ground areas I went into, all of the manhole covers were locked from the inside.

While walking around Durango I noticed five different below ground shops. These appear to be original.

Below Ground Shop Entrances
Main Avenue, Durango

Below ground shop.

The Silk Sparrow clothing store in a below ground shop.

All three photos are below ground shops in Durango.

This location has a below ground vault that did not connect to the tunnel system. On the ceiling you can see the concrete sidewalk peaking through the original wooden sidewalk.

Location Withheld
Main Avenue, Durango

Vault showing the walls, support beam, and the exposed sidewalk overhead.

Location Withheld
Main Avenue, Durango

This building has a large vault under the sidewalk. One side was used for coal delivery and the other for storage. The sidewalk can be clearly seen overhead, as well as the sagging original wooden sidewalk. A large wooden square on the ceiling seems to be the original location of an old service elevator or perhaps a large ventilation grate.

Original coal room under the sidewalk.

A vault under the sidewalk. The original sagging wooden sidewalk can be seen in the upper left corner.

This basement has two possible below ground shops. The sealed up staircase leads up to the sidewalk. At the bottom of the stairs you can turn left and enter the first shop. A large intact window can be seen at the bottom of the stairs. The second shop, to the right, has two doorways leading into it. The shop does have a locked manhole cover, but it wasn't used for the delivery of coal. A coal chute is just out of camera range. The support beams were put into place to make sure the vault was stable.

Animas Trading Company
1015 Main Avenue, Durango

The staircase leading down from the sidewalk. The window is on the left.

The original window seen at the bottom of the stairs.

The double door entrance into the second below ground shop.

The inside of the below ground shop. The locked manhole cover can be seen overhead.

The Steaming Bean

915 Main Avenue, Durango

The Steaming Bean has two doors and one window that lead either into the tunnel system or into vault rooms under the sidewalk. I was not allowed by the employees to get the door open enough to peak inside and the store's owner didn't return my calls. The size of the window indicates that this area could have been used as a below ground shop, and the store is close enough to the open tunnel system that it easily could have been part of it. This store will, unfortunately, remain a mystery.

A plywood covered doorway.

The secret doorway that might lead into the tunnel system.

A large sealed-up window.

May Palace

909 Main Avenue, Durango

This building, which was built in 1889, houses a very good Asian restaurant. We ate there during our visit to Durango and were very impressed.

In the basement we found a wonderful vault with an arched ceiling that was unfortunately full of garbage. Near the door there are two boarded-up windows, but it is unclear if this room is part of the tunnel system or simply a vault. Unfortunately, the garbage was piled high against the back walls and blocked my view. The basement also has a wonderful two-lane bowling alley that is original to the building, leading one to believe that the large vault room connected to the tunnel system.

The wooden door leading into the vault.

The vault side of the door. One of the windows can be seen.

The inside of the vault with its beautiful arched ceiling.

The original two-lane bowling alley.

TWELVE
Salida

Does Salida really have tunnels?

Were the tunnels used to visit prostitutes?

Did the tunnels go to the train depot?

Did the tunnels lead to a gym where Jack Dempsey once boxed?

The story of Salida is filled with a few name changes, a war, hurt feelings, and a lot of spite.

The first settlement in the area was the William Bale ranch. In 1874, Mr. Bale, his wife, and three daughters had a farm that quickly became a stage stop for miners headed to Leadville from Cañon City. He built additions onto his farmhouse and named it the South Arkansas Station. Soon others started to open up shop in the area, so he changed the name of his new little town to Cleora after his youngest daughter.

During the summer of 1878, due to the silver boom in Leadville, two railways were fighting to be the first to reach Leadville from Denver. The railways, the Santa Fe and the Denver & Rio Grande, were both building tracks to Leadville until they reached the Royal Gorge, just outside the town of Cañon City. Since the area was only wide enough for one set of tracks, a fight started. The Santa Fe had reached the gorge first, but the Denver & Rio Grande felt it was their right to build tracks instead and took the dispute to court. The battle was called "The Royal Gorge War."

In the spring of 1879, the court granted the rights to the Denver & Rio Grande because they had submitted a survey of the Royal Gorge area that they had done in 1872. As part of the agreement, the Denver & Rio Grande had to give up rights to Raton Pass and pay the Santa Fe Railroad for the track they had already laid.

After they won the court battle, it was time for the Denver & Rio Grande to choose train stops along the way to Leadville. The Santa Fe Railroad had already chosen Cleora as their train stop, but out of spite the Denver & Rio Grande chose a vacant piece of land only a mile and a half down the river. They named their new town South Arkansas, the original name of Cleora, to further add salt to the wound.

Not one to miss an opportunity, William Bale took his converted farmhouse and moved it to the new town of South Arkansas. Due to the size of his building, he cut it in half, placed it on logs and rolled it to its new location near the future rail yards. It took a team of eight oxen and many men to move the building. Smaller buildings and homes in Cleora were moved by placing them on wheeled carts, which were pulled by oxen or horses. The train tracks finally reached South Arkansas on May 1, 1880.

The only problem that the new town encountered was its name. It seems that after Cleora dropped their original name of South Arkansas, a small town nearby took the name for itself. Now there were two towns with the same name, and the postal service demanded that the newer town change its name. Ex-governor A.C. Hunt, who now worked for the Denver & Rio Grande Railroad, asked his wife to name the new town. She named it "Salida," to be pronounced Sa-Lee-Da. It is the Spanish word for "gateway" or "portal," because she felt it was "the portal to the riches of the surrounding world."

The first town that had used the name South Arkansas soon dropped the name and on December 8, 1880, changed its name to "Poncha Springs."

The tunnel system in Salida is one of the most intact that I have found in the state. This, I discovered, is because most of the town denies that it's there. This denial has allowed many of the tunnel entrances to remain untouched.

While doing research, I did encounter an odd man who claimed to be the town historian. When I showed him a photo I had taken of the amazing open tunnel system, he said it was a fake. His reasoning? He said, "I have been in every basement and building in this entire town. If a tunnel is going to be found, it will be found by me … not some young female!" This type of attitude might help explain the reason Salida has stayed in the dark so long.

In regards to the tunnel system going all the way to the train station, it's very unlikely. Many newspaper stories tell of taxi services, at all hours of the night, taking people home or to a hotel from the train station.

The tunnel system I found went down F Street (main street)

and turned at First Street, which is over two blocks from the train station. There was one building, the Victorian Tavern, that I was not allowed access to, which is about one block from the train station. Since I was not allowed into its basement, I can't completely rule out a tunnel entrance from their building.

Did men take the tunnels to visit prostitutes? Maybe. A lot of the "Rooms to Rent" down F Street were above the businesses that did have tunnel access. The main red light district was on Sackett Street, which is located at the end of F Street.

I did, however, discover a below ground shop that faced Sackett Street. Along with its window and door, it also had a sealed-up area that may have led into the tunnel system. With this below ground shop being located diagonally across the street from the Victorian Tavern, which I was not allowed access, I can't rule out a tunnel to the red light district or at least a tunnel from that business.

I did discover that a restaurant named "Laughing Ladies" on First Street was so named because men used the original business to

Downtown Salida in 1894. Tenderfoot Mountain can be seen in the background covered in trees, and missing the familiar "S." (Courtesy The Salida Museum)

access the red light district, located one street behind. They would walk through the front door, and then right out the back door. No tunnel needed.

When it comes to Jack Dempsey, he did box in a below ground gym on F Street. The gym was accessed via a staircase located on the sidewalk or through the tunnel system. The gym still has a faded scoreboard drawn on the wall. At the time, Jack Dempsey was working as a janitor for Madam Laura Evens and eventually married one of her girls.

With Salida being such a tourist friendly town, it would seem the logical choice for them to re-open the tunnels and the gym for tours.

These two buildings both have large basement areas. The Strait building, built in 1902, originally housed a grocery store on the first floor and the Elks Hall on the second. The basement area has been left intact and has dirt floors. A staircase, which has a strange cut taken out of it, originally led down to the basement areas. Inside the basement I found sealed-up windows, but no door. It is very possible that the door was located in the McKenna building basement next door, or perhaps the windows simply had window wells, with grates, to allow in light.

The McKenna building, which was also built in 1902, originally held a meat market and grocery store. A 1902 newspaper article reads, "The lower floor and basement are occupied by retail shops." Could these have been below ground shops accessed by the existing tunnel system?

The Strait-McKenna Buildings
230 F Street, Salida

Two sealed-up windows in the Strait building basement.

The Mixing Bowl

148 F Street, Salida

This late 1800s building housed a meat market and grocery store. The basement has a locked wooden door, a sealed-up window and an intact coal chute. The back wall of the basement was covered over after an intense remodel to shore up the foundation, so it is unknown if any tunnel access existed in that part of the basement.

The bricked-in window.

The locked wooden door that led into the tunnel system.

This building, which originally housed a grocery store, appears to have been built around 1886. The A.T Henry building, built in 1886 and located across the street, is the same style and design as this building. Unfortunately, the beautiful decorative trim on the roof of the Culture Clash building was destroyed in a fire, which resulted in the plain roof we see today.

These two buildings are connected by a tunnel that originally went underneath F Street. The A.T. Henry building was originally the Chaffee County Bank, and a tunnel would have allowed business owners to access the bank without the chance of being robbed. A second tunnel went underneath First Street and connected to the building that houses Krivanek Jewelers at 101 F Street. This building originally housed a drug store and the Continental Divide Bank. When I investigated the building's two shops, Krivanek Jewelers and Cowgirl Coffee, I discovered that one no longer had basement access for the front of the building and the other had been remodeled.

The Culture Clash building houses a wonderfully intact below ground shop, which rumor has it used to be a barbershop. The shop contains four windows and two doors. The first door, located at the bottom of the stairs, is used to access the below ground shop from street level. The second door, which is painted three different colors, leads to the tunnels. The access, which is behind the staircase, has been bricked over. If you look closely, you can see the original brickwork near the ceiling. All four windows can be seen inside the shop, with two of them facing a narrow tunnel. This tunnel appears to have been used to allow light into the windows through sidewalk grates, not as a walk through tunnel. This tunnel area is only three feet wide, where a regular tunnel is normally five feet wide. The original windows, with some glass still intact, can be seen.

Outside the below ground shop, but still inside the basement, I discovered an odd, small doorway. This doorway leads to the shop next door, 105 North F Street, which has two entrances into its basement. This shop, which is located in the same building as Culture Clash, has a stairway that leads from the main floor and a stairway that leads from the basement to an outside doorway. While interviewing Salida natives, I was told that the shop at 105 North F Street used to be a shoeshine shop. It was also used as the entrance into the tunnel system, as long as you gave the "gatekeeper" the right password.

Culture Clash
101 North F Street, Salida

The outside entrance to the below ground shop. The two windows and the door can be seen leading into the below ground shop outside of Culture Clash.

Inside the below ground shop. The original woodwork, wainscoting, and wallpaper can be seen.

Two windows inside the below ground shop. Through the broken glass you can see the smaller tunnel.

The second door, which leads to the tunnels.

The two bricked-over tunnel entrances. The original brick can be seen near the ceiling.

The odd little door that leads to the building next door.

First Colorado Land Office

202 North F Street, Salida

This building was built in 1904 as part of the Palace Hotel and originally housed a restaurant. The building faces F Street in the front and Sackett Street from the side. It is the Sackett Street side that contains a below ground shop entrance. The shop contains one window, one door, and a sealed-up area in the back, which may have led into the tunnel system. If this is true, then a tunnel system "might" have connected to the red light district that was also located on Sackett Street. The large, beige building located in the upper left hand corner of the photo is the Parlor House.

I was unable to get into the basement of the First Colorado Land Office, but I was able to get into the basement of the Palace Hotel's main building. Inside I was shown that all the walls had been plastered over and remodeled.

Parlor House

The below ground shop with a gate.

The Salida Opera House opened on New Years day in 1890, but it wasn't Salida's first opera house. The first opera house was named the Dickmann's Opera House and was located on the corner of 2nd Street and F Street. It was later re-named the Craig's Opera House, but it burned down on January 2nd, during the fire of 1888.

In 1909, the Salida Opera House was re-named the Osos Grand Theater and showed not only plays, but movies. In 1936, the building was again re-named and became the Salida Theater, and began only showing movies. In the 1960s the building received its current name, the Unique Theater, which closed in August 2006.

The building not only includes the main theater, but two storefronts. One was not accessible through the theater's main lobby, but the second one was. This storefront originally was a restaurant and lounge for the theater patrons. It was inside this store's basement that I found a tunnel entrance.

Down a well-built staircase, I entered a room with trash and dirt covering the original wooden floors. On the back wall I discovered the locked wooden door that led into the tunnel system. Just a couple doors down from the theater is the Sherman Hotel. A tunnel, leading into the theater, would have been a very convenient way to see a show in bad weather, or to visit the ladies of the evening who are rumored to have rented rooms at the Sherman Hotel. Unfortunately, the Sherman Hotel sealed up most of their basement, so I was unable to access it.

The Unique Theater (Salida Opera House)
129 West First Street, Salida

The locked wooden door in the basement of the Unique Theater.

Beadsong
107 F Street

Mountain Vista Properties
115A F Street

Fat Tees
115B F Street

Seasons Celebrations
117 F Street, Salida

These four stores are located inside the Sweet building, which was built in 1886. It originally housed a drug store, clothing store, and fruit market. All four stores have wonderful tunnel access, with intact doors and windows. A photo taken of the building in the late 1800s shows the original grates on the wooden sidewalk, which allowed fresh air and sunlight into the tunnel areas.

The basement tunnel accesses are all similar, with matching doors, doorknobs, hinges, windows, and large open basements—except Seasons Celebrations. Their basement staircase is very narrow and their basement appeared to only be around 12x12 square feet. They also have a very ornate door and window, which is much fancier than the other three. Unfortunately, Seasons Celebrations wouldn't allow me to take pictures.

This building's tunnel system would be one of the easiest to re-open and give tours of. It's in wonderful condition.

Late 1800s photo of the building showing the grates on the wooden sidewalk. (Courtesy The Salida Museum)

A boarded-up window that shows the boards nailed from the outside.

A locked door and boarded-up window.

These stores are all located inside the original Crews-Beggs building, built in 1900. Crews-Beggs was a dry goods company founded in Leadville by Charles Weber Crews and his uncle, R.H. Beggs.

This building, thanks to the owner of Monarch Brokers, has an amazing, intact tunnel—the best in the state. The open tunnel system is sixty feet long, five feet wide, and almost seven feet tall. It has two doorways and six sealed-up windows. This area could have been used for below ground shops due to the fancy stone windowsills and arched doorways, or simply elaborate storage rooms. Considering how close this area is to the below ground gym, I'm leaning more toward below ground shops.

A photo taken in 1900 shows the grates on the sidewalk that allowed light and air into the basement. These were placed above the windows so that when the windows were open, fresh air could enter the basement areas. Natives of Salida told me that even in the 1950s the sidewalk would still light up at night from those grates, and you could see right into the tunnels.

Monarch Brokers
203 F Street

Handlebars Barbershop
207 F Street

Sunshine Market
211 F Street, Salida

A 1900 photo showing the grates on the sidewalk.
(Courtesy The Salida Museum)

A Salida resident, who used to work in the building as a teenager when it was Binns Grocery, told me how they used the tunnels to store potatoes and onions. As you walk down the steps into the basement, you can see on the wall where he signed his name on September 29, 1937. The earliest name on the wall is for Harold Clyde Binns on March 8, 1919. The resident has heard that the area was called "The Gallery," and you needed a password to come downstairs, after dark, to play poker. This would make sense, considering that the tunnel connects to the below ground gym that houses the boxing ring where Jack Dempsey used to fight.

At the end of the tunnel, you see a brick wall. If you stand on a chair and peak over the brick wall, you can see the remainder of the tunnel system that leads to the gym.

My assistants standing in the open tunnel system. The brace helps to hold up the sidewalk. This was my daughter's first tunnel, and she was a little nervous.

The sealed-up windows with stone windowsills.

The brick wall that blocks the entrance into the gym.

Pinon Real Estate Group

201 F Street, Salida

The Knights of Pythias building was built in 1895. The ground floor housed the First National Bank until 1934 and the second floor was the meeting room for The Knights of Pythias, which was a fraternal organization for the Denver & Rio Grande Railroad workers. The second floor still houses odd characteristics, such as six-foot-high closets stacked on top of each other and peepholes in the doors.

Being a building that housed a bank, it's unexpected to find a large below ground gym in the basement. The only current access into the basement is a small, narrow staircase that is hidden inside a closet ... in the bathroom ... behind the door.

You then enter the underground tunnel system with its amazing arched ceilings and visible manhole covers. This tunnel goes down the entire side of the building, which faces 2nd Street. The tunnel is bricked up at the back of the building. When you enter the gym, it surprises you by its size. The bricked-in windows are over seven feet tall and the gym itself is almost ten feet tall. An old scoreboard is still drawn on the wall.

Going through the door against the back wall, you come to a small part of the tunnel system that is sealed off at both ends. One end is brick, which if removed, would continue into the tunnel shared by Monarch Brokers next door. The opposite end is a sealed-up tunnel entrance that originally continued under the sidewalk, but only to 2nd Street, which it did not go under. This area is eighteen feet long, seven feet high, and five feet wide.

Going back out of the gym and into the first tunnel system there is a set of original stairs that lead outside. Going around them you come to a sealed-up rock wall. This wall is the closed-off portion of the tunnel that went under F Street to the Wenz building, which was torn down in the 1980s. My assistant and I stood on a chair and removed a stone from the top of the wall, which is stacked but not mortared, and found proof that the tunnel continues under the street.

This building, along with the tunnel system located between 107–117 F Street, would be simple to restore and open for tours. This would be a wonderful way to bring more tourism into Salida. Treasures like these should be shared, not hidden.

The tunnel system that runs down 2nd Street.

The tunnel system with a manhole cover in the front.

The inside of the same tunnel system. The sealed-up window can be seen with the original grate still intact, but covered over.

The removed stone from the sealed-up tunnel showing how the tunnel continues under F Street

The original staircase inside the tunnel. The original metal door can be seen above.

One of two, seven-foot tall, sealed-up windows of the gym. The door into the tunnel system can be seen.

THIRTEEN
Cañon City

Does Cañon City have tunnels?

Does the Holy Cross Abbey have tunnels?

Did the KKK use the tunnels to travel through downtown?

Is there really a tunnel from Cañon City to Florence?

Does Cañon City have below ground shops?

Did Cañon City have a tunnel to the train depot?

Cañon City has had its share of founders and its share of Indians stealing laundry ... but it still went on to be a town that Theodore Roosevelt himself was proud of.

The area was first founded by Lieutenant Zebulon Pike on December 8, 1806. His party was looking for the source of the Arkansas River, which they didn't find. Surprisingly, they did find a sulphur spring he named "Vichy Waters," after Vichy, France, which is a spa and resort town known for its mineral water. Zebulon Pike's cottonwood log cabin was the first structure built in the area. He left the area on January 14, 1807.

Nobody showed any real interest in the area again until 1859, when the gold rush came. Josiah F. Young, Robert Bercaw, Charles D. Peck, and William Kroenig, all from Pueblo, liked the area and felt it would be a "Great natural thoroughfare for gold seekers." They platted out the town and named it Cañon City, after the large canyons in the area. Unfortunately, when winter came, all the men except William Kroenig abandoned the new town.

Kroenig, in an attempt to save the town, contacted Buell and Boyd, two Denver engineers, who platted out the town's 1,280 acres, lost interest, and left.

In 1862, Governor Gilpin sent Anson Rudd, J.B. Cooper, and Lewis Conley to draft out the boundaries of Fremont County, but by the spring of 1863, Cañon City was once again abandoned, this time due to the Civil War.

Anson Rudd and his wife were positive that people would soon return to Cañon City, and they wanted to make sure the town was in tip-top shape when they did. They guarded the empty town for over a year. The only other resident they had was an insane woman who lived for a short time in one of the abandoned cabins. She called herself the "Queen of Sheba" and would rant about the Devil.

On August 13, 1864, twenty families, who called themselves the Resurrectionists, pulled into town from Omaha, Nebraska. They were part of the Polish Resurrection Order, a religious group founded in Paris in 1836 and based on Roman Catholic beliefs. This group included Thomas and Joseph Macon and Mrs. Anna Harrison and her three sons. The new residents re-opened the stores and the town came back to life. The town was incorporated in 1872.

The town was located in Indian territory and the Ute Indians were a real bother to the residents of Cañon City. They would beg and steal, but luckily caused no real harm. Mrs. Rudd reported how she had found four Indian braves sitting on her floor watching her iron clothes. Mrs. Blakeslee found four Indians in her kitchen begging for food. She fed them and later found that they had stolen all her clothes off the clothesline. Benjamin Griffin told of a visit from Chief Colorow who insisted on drinking from a bottle on the table. Mr. Griffin tried to explain that it was medicine for his cows, but the chief insisted on drinking it. After the burning stopped, he said, "Give me bottle. Me take to camp, have fun with braves."

Cañon City received a pleasant surprise on May 8, 1905, when ex-President Theodore Roosevelt visited the town during a vacation in Colorado. During a speech he said, "I want to say how pleased I am to go through your state and see its resources. Not only your mines, your fruit and all its products, but I want to say you have got a wonderful asset in your scenery, in the natural beauties of this state."

In regards to the tunnels, the silliest rumor I have heard has to be that there is a tunnel from Cañon City to Florence. This would require a tunnel to be built under the Arkansas River and the towns are also over eight miles apart. There is no need or reason for this to exist, and it doesn't.

There are also many rumors of the Ku Klux Klan building tunnels to sneak around town and into the Holy Cross Abbey. History shows that the Cañon City branch of the KKK had no need to sneak around, as the members were all very open about their membership and even hung signs in their stores. The KKK started in Cañon City on January 31, 1924, in an attempt to stop the construction of the Holy Cross Abbey. The Benedictine monks had purchased the land in 1923, which angered the klan. The klan disliked the Catholics because they believed they worshiped the Pope and that was un-American. The KKK surprisingly left the black residents alone, mostly because they were Baptists. Fred Arnold, the local Baptist minister, was the "Exalted Cyclops" for the Cañon City branch of the KKK.

Despite all the hype, the KKK did very little to stop the construction of the abbey. They once burned a cross on the lawn during construction and forced the local lumberyard to refuse the purchase of supplies. The stones used in the construction of the abbey were delivered at night by train and placed on the future abbey grounds. To make construction easier, all the stones were numbered. To try to prevent the construction of the abbey, the KKK would sneak onto the grounds and re-arrange the stones.

Cañon City in the early 1900s. (Courtesy Royal Gorge Regional Museum & History Center)

The KKK posing on a Ferris wheel April 26, 1926. (Courtesy Royal Gorge Regional Museum & History Center)

The KKK met in the back room of the St. Cloud Hotel, which was behind the Baptist church. They had no need for tunnels. When the Baptist minister died in 1928, interest in the KKK in Cañon City died with him.

I have also heard many stories of tunnels leading from the prison, located at the end of Main Street. These are not the types of tunnels I researched and I will not put the prison at risk by documenting those types of tunnels, if they do indeed exist.

The Holy Cross Abbey
2951 East U.S. Highway 50, Cañon City

The abbey was constructed between 1924 and 1926 at a cost of $500,000. In today's market, that is over six million dollars. The abbey was built for the Order of St. Benedict and the Benedictine monks. It housed a school for boys until it closed in 1985 due to poor enrollment.

The abbey does not have tunnels and it never did. I am including it in this chapter only to banish the rumors once and for all.

When I toured the abbey, I was shown the area that has been rumored to be the tunnel entrance. It is simply a false floor in a closet in the basement. This is where the students would hide their liquor stash and other treasures from the staff. All of the articles pulled out of the closet were dated from the 1980s. If this really was a tunnel entrance into the boys dorms, it would not be located in the floor of a closet, but on the back wall. It also wouldn't be in a small closet, but in a large open walkway or large sealed-up doorway.

I have also interviewed many former students of the abbey, including one man who went from being a student in the 1940s to a priest who then worked there until it closed. He told me how the abbey had to be jacked up and stabilized in the 1960s due to the bad soil. He watched as the workers dug a trench eight to ten feet deep all the way around the building. The abbey was then jacked up and concrete pylons were poured four to five feet apart. Concrete was then poured in the trenches and covered with dirt. He said that he never saw a tunnel or anything that could ever have been a tunnel during the construction.

All the former students I interviewed said the same thing in regards to the tunnels. "I wish there had been, it would have made the walk easier in the winter."

The closet that was rumored to hold the tunnel.

Haley's Cañon Western Wear

502 Main Street, Cañon City

This building, which was built in 1887, is called the Burrage building. It was built by C.W. Burrage and his brother and it housed the C.H. Whitmore and Company furniture store. This building had two below ground shops accessed by an outside staircase, which has since been sealed up. The shops originally housed the first post office, a printing shop, and a shoe repair shop.

Inside the basement, I was able to see the original door and window and noticed that the outside staircase has not been filled in with dirt, as I could see through the glass of the original window. Unfortunately, the store's owner would not allow me to open the door, so I cannot say if the open stairway leads to a tunnel system.

The original door, still intact.

The original window, still intact.

This building, which was built around 1877, originally housed the Alling Hardware Company. The side of the building facing 4th Street has an exposed tunnel with two doors and two windows. I was refused access to the basement area, but was told that it had been drywalled over on the inside … and I was also told that it wasn't. Regardless, the end of the tunnel has a concreted over doorway that may have led into the tunnel system. This building is diagonally across from the Strathmore Hotel, which does have below ground shops. It is possible that they may have connected.

Bresnan Communications
402 Main Street, Cañon City

The open tunnel with two doorways and two windows.

Anita McCoy Dance Studio
724 Main Street

Empty Store
722 Main Street, Cañon City

This building, which was built around 1904, originally housed many offices and businesses. It also housed three below ground shops, but they were not accessed from the outside. The inside of the building originally had a large staircase that led down from the first floor to a basement landing. At this point you turned either left or right. The left side held one shop, while the right side held two.

The second shop on the right side housed the Westinghouse Mazda Lamps Lighting Service, as seen advertised on the shop's original door. Mazda brand lightbulbs were in use from 1909 to 1945, so it's hard to truly date when the store was in use.

This building also has two metal grates, with crystals, on the sidewalk. These grates do not let light into a tunnel system, but instead into two window wells.

The original staircase that led to the below ground shops.

One of two doors that led into the shops. The basement landing can be seen behind the door.

One of two crystal-filled grates outside the building.

An inside view of the crystal-filled grates.

The McClure-Strathmore Hotel

331 Main Street, Cañon City

This building, which opened on October 4, 1864, was built on the former site of Anson Rudd's log cabin blacksmith shop. It not only housed elegant hotel rooms, but also several businesses. These included the Fremont County Bank, the *Cañon City Daily Record,* a saloon, and a drug store. Despite all the glamour, the hotel caused its builder, William H. McClure, financial ruin.

As a unique feature, the hotel was built with four below ground shops called "The Arcade." It housed a barbershop, a billiard parlor, a shoe store, and a hardware store. The stores were accessed by an outside staircase located on the sidewalk on the Main Street side of the building.

Unfortunately, despite numerous attempts, I was refused access to the basement of the building. Luckily, the local museum was allowed access many years ago, but surprisingly, took only four pictures. One picture shows what appears to be a sealed-off tunnel facing Main Street. Now the questions and rumors started.

Did the tunnel lead to the train station? All the evidence I have found leads me to believe it did not. I was given a tour of the basement area of the train depot and it is only a small room holding a boiler and plumbing equipment. I was also informed that the ground was too wet and muddy to have supported a tunnel that close to the river.

Did the tunnel possibly end at the old fire department at 330 Royal Gorge Boulevard and then was a bridge built for people to simply walk the rest of the way to the train depot? The old fire department building, which does have a suspicious-looking concrete wall that faces the train depot, was not built until 1939. Before 1939, the area between the hotel and the train depot contained houses … so no tunnel.

Also, in 1905, the Strathmore Hotel advertised that they had a horse-drawn carriage that met all the trains and picked up guests. If the hotel had a tunnel system, the carriages would not have been needed.

I did interview an elderly native of Cañon City, who told me a story about the store across the street from the Strathmore Hotel. The building, which was built around 1888, originally housed a meat market. The man told me how, in 1923, his father-in-law George Batchelor bought the building and turned it into a dairy processing business. His father-in-law told him stories of how he had found an open tunnel in the basement that led across the street to the Strathmore Hotel. The original owner had informed Batchelor that the tunnel was used to deliver meat to the hotel. Around 1940, Batchelor sealed up the tunnel opening in order to use the basement area for more refrigerators.

Could this be the real use for the sealed-up tunnel entrance found in the Strathmore's below ground shop area or is it really just a shoeshine booth like the museum has it listed?

The metal grate filled with crystals.

The metal grate seen from inside the tunnel. (Courtesy Royal Gorge Regional Museum & History Center)

An original window advertising shoes for the shoe store. (Courtesy Royal Gorge Regional Museum & History Center)

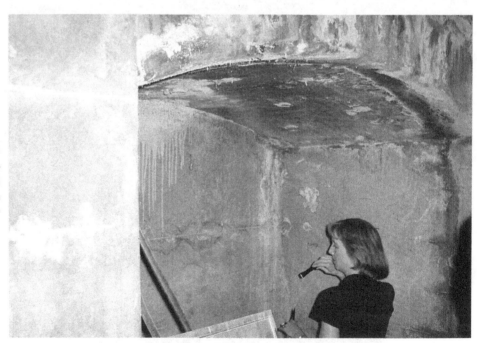

The sealed-off tunnel entrance or a shoeshine booth? (Courtesy Royal Gorge Regional Museum & History Center)

FOURTEEN

Florence

Does Florence have tunnels?

Does Florence have any below ground shops?

Are the tunnels simply the old steam pipes?

Did Florence help save the victims of the Ludlow Massacre?

Did Florence help save the victims of the 1899 Victor fire?

The history of Florence started with apples, continued with oil and coal, and has become one of the largest gathering places of antique dealers in the state. And unbeknownst to most people, Florence's train engineers have risked their lives to save thousands of people.

In 1861, a man named Jessie Frazer discovered the area and found that it was full of rich soil. He went back home to St. Louis, Missouri, hooked up his team of oxen, and filled up his wagon with two thousand apple tree seedlings. He planted the first orchard along the Arkansas River, and possibly the first orchard in Colorado.

In 1869, a man named James A. McCandless visited the area and decided it would be a great place for a town due to all the farms. On June 4, 1870, he bought three hundred and twenty acres of land from Issac W. Chatfield and his wife for $5,000. In November 1872, he hired Townshend S. Brandegee to plat out the area for the town, which included thirty acres. It was then discovered that the area had already been platted by the Denver & Rio Grande Railroad and that the railroad had purchased land about a quarter mile from where McCandless had platted his town. The railroad had discussed naming the area LaBran, but had never filed the name. The town was named Florence after McCandless's daughter, Minnie Florence McCandless. The town boomed and was incorporated on August 11, 1887.

McCandless saw opportunity in the Cripple Creek and Victor gold mines and founded the Florence and Cripple Creek Railroad. This would allow the delivery of gold ore from Cripple Creek, and the area he chose for the track was called Phantom Canyon. Due to the narrow mountain canyon, he used a narrow gauge track of two feet wide rather than the standard gauge track of four feet, eight and a half inches.

In August 1899, Florence received word that the town of Victor, located five miles south of Cripple Creek, was engulfed in flames. Train engineers quickly headed the train up Phantom Canyon and used the empty train cars to load up the town's residents and all the goods that could be saved. The train then backed up the mountain and stopped. The town's residents sat in safety as they watched their town burn. The entire business district was lost.

On April 20, 1914, the town of Florence received word that the mining camp of Ludlow was under threat from the Colorado National Guard due to a mining strike. Train engineers quickly headed toward Ludlow—over one hundred miles away. It was dusk when they arrived to find a terrible sight. The entire mining camp, which included twelve hundred miners plus their wives and children, were being massacred. The Baldwin Felts Detective Agency had supplied an armored car with a mounted machine gun and, along with the National Guard, were firing on the residents.

The train conductor noticed that the train tracks separated the armored car from the camp. Making a life or death decision, he pulled the train into the line of fire to block the machine gun. Many of the miners and their families quickly loaded into the train cars as the train began to be fired upon. Due to the risk to the train, it couldn't completely stop, but simply slowed down to a crawl. If they would have stopped, the damage to the engine and the train cars from the machine gun would have been too severe for them to be able to evacuate. The camp's residents were taken back to Florence.

In all, between eighteen and twenty-five miners were murdered and thirteen women and children were burned to death when their tents were doused with kerosene and set on fire. A twelve-year-old boy named Frank Snyder was shot and killed while trying to save his kitten. None of the two hundred-plus perpetrators were ever convicted.

Florence in 1904. (Courtesy Denver Public Library Western History Collection, #MCC-1892)

The 1899 Victor fire. The train from Florence can be seen piled high with clothing and furniture. (Courtesy Denver Public Library Western History Collection, #X-540)

The Smokestack
Florence

One of the most popular rumors regarding tunnels in Florence are the smokestacks. Located just outside of town, the two remaining smokestacks do have tunnels, but not for sneaking around town. These smokestacks supplied steam heat for local businesses. The insides of the tunnels are accessed through a broken section of brick, which is not the original entrance. The property manager, who took my assistant and me for a tour, said that the insides have been filled in with dirt many times to keep out teenagers, but they still sneak in. The tunnels are not big enough to stand in and they no longer lead into town or supply heat.

It is possible that when the smokestacks were no longer in use that people snuck around in them, but that was not the tunnels' intention. There are no vents for fresh air or light and it gets really stuffy and dark in there.

Broken entrance into the smokestack tunnels.

My assistant posing inside the tunnel.

This building was built by Phillip Griffith in 1894 and housed a saloon, feed store, and later an Eagles Hall. The building has an outside entrance into the basement with a very fancy door, complete with a transom window. There are also four other windows in the basement with window wells that originally had metal grates for ventilation and to allow in light. It is felt by some that the area may have been a below ground shop or a gentlemen's club.

The Florence Pioneer Museum
100 East Front Street, Florence

The outside entrance into the below ground area.

The door into the below ground area.

One of the four window wells—this one now houses a taxidermied skunk.

McCandless Building

109–111 Main Street,
Florence

This building opened on December 1, 1894, after taking almost four years to build. The first floor was originally used as a mercantile and the second and third floors were advertised as a "European Hotel." In reality, the hotel was used as a brothel and is still intact. The third floor of the brothel is open to the second floor and the roof has a large skylight. All the "girls' rooms" are just as they left them. Each room has its own door with transom window and its own "viewing window." This allowed the girls to advertise to perspective clients without leaving their room. The staircase to the two upper floors starts from the first floor and not from the sidewalk.

In the basement I did not find the rumored tunnel entrance, but I did find five large, sealed-up windows. The large windows simply let light into the basement area and at one time had grates. The basement area does have finished walls and original wallpaper, so it may have been used as a basement store.

There is a hole in the corner of the basement, through a window opening. When I crawled up, I could see the sidewalk and the opening appears to be less than three feet wide. If this were a tunnel, it would be a minimum of five feet wide. The size indicates it was simply used for sidewalk grates, not a tunnel.

The inside of the brothel.

Two sealed-up windows. The original wallpaper can be seen.

Looking through the exposed hole. The sidewalk can be seen.

Florence Flower Shop

105 West Main Street,
Florence

The Castle Hall building was built by the Knights of Pythias and opened in September 1887. It housed Petroleum Lodge 36, which was the first American Fraternal Order chartered by an act of Congress. The basement housed a theater open to the public and accessed from an outside stairway. An article in the *Oil Refiner* newspaper reports that the Knights of Pythias were remodeling the basement for a show. The historic newspaper also showed a photo of the outside of the building. It had two sidewalk entrances down into the basement, one from the left and one from the right, with metal railings. The center was left as a stairway into the store on the ground floor. The condition of this photo was very poor quality and I opted not to use it.

The basement had three windows with window wells on the west side of the building. This area was a small "muleway alley" built between two buildings. This type of alley was built just wide enough for a mule with a full pack to walk through. The building originally had a stable in the back. The grates were removed and the window wells covered up in 1900.

The theater was open until the 1921 flood, when it filled with water. After the water was pumped out, the decision was made to close the theater. The front was bricked in and sealed up.

The basement theater. The back wall has been covered over, but the outline of the original windows can be seen. Part of the original wood floor can also be seen.

One of the three windows.

The hotel, built in 1901, was not the only hotel in town. The Florence Hotel, which was at 100 Main Street, opened in 1890. Due to the name, this hotel simply switched the words around ... and became the Hotel Florence. The building also originally housed a café on the first floor.

This building houses a below ground shop, which you enter by going down the stairs and entering the door to the right. The secret comes from the sealed-up doorway you encounter at the foot of the stairs. During an interview with the building's owner, he informed me that a vault does exist below the sidewalk and that the manhole cover, which used to hold crystals, helped light up that area. A large grate on the sidewalk, which can be seen just past the staircase, was the original coal chute. With the doorway filled in and the vault's entrance bricked over inside the building's basement, we may never know if this building holds a tunnel to the train station located just a block behind the hotel. I don't feel the tunnel would have gone across the street to 131B because that building was originally a hardware store and there wouldn't have been a reason to connect the two.

The below ground shop was originally used as a gentlemen's club and more recently was a ceramic shop.

Hotel Florence
201 Main Street, Florence

A sealed-up doorway leading to a vault under the sidewalk.

A manhole cover with most of its crystals missing.

The below ground shop entrance.

Lovell Block
132 Main Street, Florence

This building, which was built in 1894, was originally the Lewis and Yost Dry Goods. More recently, it housed the Main Street Grill. I was unable to get into the basement. From the sidewalk you can see two grates that are covering over window wells.

A window well with the original grate.

This 1890 building originally housed the Florence Hotel. The first floor was used as offices and the Green Lantern Saloon. The hotel was used mainly as a boarding house, where many traveling salesmen would stay. This building has a below ground shop entrance and two sealed-up window wells. I was refused entrance into the basement.

Cañon National Bank
100 Main Street, Florence

Below ground entrance covered with a locked grate. (Courtesy author's collection)

This building, which was built in two parts, was built between 1897 and 1900. Called the Wilson block or Wilson annex, it was originally built with the Lennox Hotel on the second floor and a hardware store and Barry's Grocery on the first floor.

The west side of this building has five window wells with metal grates. I was unable to gain access to the basement, but I could see the intact windows through the grates and see that they were only window wells and not part of a tunnel.

Good Stuff Antiques
131 B Main Street, Florence

Five window wells with original grates.

Empty Building
107 Front Street, Florence

This 1895 building is in the McDonald block. The building was originally a print shop on the first floor, rooms to rent on the second floor, and the Union Laundry in the below ground shop. Later the building was used as a macaroni factory and a bottling works. I love the architecture of this building, and the small bridge going over the below ground shop is wonderful.

This building was vacant, so I was unable to access the below ground shop.

The outside of the empty building.

The entrance to the below ground shop.
Notice the bridge to the first floor.

FIFTEEN
Trinidad

Does Trinidad have tunnels?

Is there really a tunnel under the whole town?

Was Main Street raised up after the 1903 flood?

Did Al Capone dig a tunnel from Trinidad to Aguilar?

The town of Trinidad has a history dating back to the 1840s and the Santa Fe Trail. Commercial Street follows the original Santa Fe Trial, which was created by caravans crossing the river. This trail crosses over an older trail, where Main Street is now. This intersection was once the camping grounds where wagons would stop before tackling Raton Pass.

The journey up Raton Pass took about a week and there was always the fear of a wagon going over the edge and crashing into the ravine. This is why most of the early wagon trains took the Cimarron cutoff, which crossed the Oklahoma and New Mexico plains. This trail was dangerous due to Indian attacks and the lack of water. In later years, a man named Uncle Dick Wooton built a toll road over Raton Pass and people were threatened at gunpoint to pay the toll.

The first permanent settlement was started in the late 1850s and the town of Trinidad was staked out in 1862. The town hit its peak in 1910 when rich veins of high-grade coking coal were discovered above Trinidad. Thousands of miners were brought in from southern Europe, Poland, Germany, Ireland, Italy, and Asia to work the mines.

The downtown businesses in Trinidad are built on the historic sites of the trading posts, stables, inns, and campsites of the Santa Fe Trail. Every day the people of Trinidad follow the exact path of the historic wagon trails.

When it comes to the tunnels under Trinidad, they are not what people expect. When I interviewed people in Trinidad, I kept hearing the story of a large drainage ditch that runs under Main Street. I was told that this "tunnel" is full of doors that allow access to the underground tunnel system … it doesn't. I walked the entire length of this ditch with both of my assistants and all we found were rocks and garbage.

I then heard people say that the entire downtown area had been raised up one level due to the 1903 and 1930s floods. Many residents feel that the below ground shop areas are simply the original ground floors of the downtown buildings … they're not. My husband and I took many pictures of the current downtown buildings from the same angle as historic Trinidad photographs and it's very obvious that the downtown buildings have not been raised. Also, in the old historic photos the below ground entrances can be seen.

Then there is the story of the tunnel that runs from Aguilar to Trinidad, used by the famous 1920s mobster Al Capone. This tunnel was supposedly built by out of work coal miners and was large enough to fit a model-T pickup. This would allow Al Capone to transport moonshine from one town to another. Capone also was

Historic downtown Trinidad in the late 1800s. (Courtesy Trinidad Public Library)

rumored to have purchased houses in Aguilar and Walsenburg to use as safe houses when the police were looking for him and his men in Chicago.

While it is possible that Al Capone did purchase houses, it is not possible nor would it have been worthwhile for him to have a tunnel dug between the two towns. Aguilar is twenty-one miles from Trinidad and if he really purchased safe houses in the area, he wouldn't want to be attracting attention by digging a tunnel from one small town to another … through a mountain. He would have simply driven the moonshine there or used the train.

When it comes to underground tunnels downtown, they do exist, but they were not always covered over. The town had many open below ground shop areas and a small walking bridge that would allow access to the first floor shops. In later years, the below ground shops were covered over with a sidewalk, which gave the impression that they were "tunnels." Since the 1980s, some of these below ground shops have been opened up and are starting to be restored.

Historic downtown Trinidad. Below ground shop entrances with metal railings can be seen in the lower right hand corner. (Courtesy Trinidad Public Library)

A current photo of the same street showing that the street has not been raised.

This building, built in 1889, houses an entire row of below ground shops. These shops were re-opened in the 1980s and are starting to be restored. An open staircase leads down to the shops, which are very well preserved. Looking down the walkway it is easy to see why the area appeared to be a tunnel once the sidewalk was placed over the top. The small bridges can be seen overhead, which allow people to enter the first floor shops.

Historic Building
319 West Main Street, Trinidad

The stairs down to the below ground shops.

One of the storefronts with original windows.

The below ground walkway. The small bridges can be seen overhead and the walkway appears to continue down the sidewalk through the sealed-up doorway.

This building, which did not wish to be identified, houses a below ground shop. The original doorway has been removed and sealed up with cinder blocks, but the window frames are still intact. To the side of the below ground shop is a wonderful double door that leads to the building next door.

Address Withheld
Main Street, Trinidad

One of the original window frames.

The wonderful double door that leads to the shop next door.

Mission at the Bell
(Mexican restaurant)
134 West Main Street,
Trinidad

This building's below ground shop has been given a facelift, but still keeps its original look. The sidewalks that originally covered over the below ground shop were removed and replaced with skylights. The original storefront was also removed and the space used to expand the restaurant. At one end there is a door that would have originally led to more below ground shops, but is sealed up. This below ground shop was originally a pool hall.

This building also has an interesting feature that almost got a mention in the *Guinness Book of World Records.* In the 1930s, famous photographer Glenn Aultman's mother bought a rubber tree plant at a local store called Cress's. The plant struggled to live in his photography studio until he decided to have it planted on the lower level of the building in 1991. At that time it was only ten feet tall. The plant now towers at fifty feet tall and is supported by the staircase it grows around. The skylight was added to the roof of the building just for the plant. When the plant was nominated for the *Guinness Book,* it was refused because the plant was not native to Colorado.

The skylight that was installed over the originally open below ground shop area.

The rubber tree plant with its personal skylight. (Courtesy Rosemary Fabec)

SIXTEEN

Colorado Springs

Does Colorado Springs have tunnels?

Does a tunnel go from the courthouse to the YWCA?

Did they really store bodies in the tunnels during the 1918 flu epidemic?

The area was founded by General William Jackson Palmer in the mid-1800s when he was scouting the best path for the Kansas-Pacific Railway. The railroad wanted to extend their tracks from Denver to the Pacific Coast, but as Palmer looked around he imagined that the area could be so much more. He envisioned opening up a resort with people soaking in the soda springs and breathing the mountain air.

When the railway rejected his route, he quit his job and decided to build his own railroad and develop the area himself. The railroad would extend south from the stopping point of the Kansas-Pacific in Denver down into Mexico. He founded the town of Colorado Springs in 1871.

Due to the large amount of British visitors and settlers, his new town was nicknamed "Little London." Soon, people started to visit the area for help with their tuberculosis. Not wanting to miss an opportunity, Palmer had two young doctors circulate rumors that the mineral springs in Manitou could cure a wide range of disorders. Soon people came from all over Europe to get healed.

Palmer also decided that his "Fountain Colony" would only be open to persons of good character and temperance habits. He also prohibited the sale of liquor within the city limits. By 1890, the town had eleven thousand residents.

In 1891, gold was discovered in Cripple Creek and millions of dollars began to flow into Colorado Springs. By 1900, Colorado Springs had twenty-one thousand residents.

When it comes to tunnels, Colorado Springs had a lot of them. Unfortunately, most have been sealed up. I heard story after story from building owners about where the tunnels were and how they sealed them up. I was lucky to find the two I did.

General Palmer staking out Colorado Springs in 1870. Palmer is in the middle with the hat and beard. The location is the future site of the Broadmoor Hotel. (Courtesy Old Colorado City Historical Society)

Colorado Springs in 1957. The original Antlers Hotel can be seen in the background. (Courtesy Old Colorado City Historical Society)

A store with grates and a below ground shop in the bottom left of the picture.
(Courtesy author's personal collection)

The Underground Bar
(Formally the YWCA)
110 North Nevada,
Colorado Springs

This building was built in October 1913, as the YWCA. The basement area has two tunnel entrances that lead out to Nevada Avenue. The area in the basement is rumored to have been a locker room due to its original tile floors.

Another rumor is that there used to be a tunnel that ran in front of the courthouse on Nevada. This tunnel, as the story goes, also ran beneath Nevada and connected to the tunnel system in front of the YWCA. When I checked, I was told that there was a sealed-up doorway in the basement of the courthouse facing Nevada Avenue, but I was not allowed to photograph it.

I also interviewed a former employee of the Public Works Department. He said he was doing major roadwork in the late 1970s or early '80s on Nevada Avenue. He discovered a spooky looking, broken down tunnel that went from the courthouse, beneath Nevada Avenue, and over to the area under the sidewalk in front of the YWCA.

In regards to people storing bodies in the tunnels, it did happen. The building next door to the YWCA was a mortuary and during the 1918 flu pandemic things got very crowded. The flu hit Colorado in September 1918 and lasted until June 1919. In all, 7,783 people died in Colorado alone and the worst months were also some of the coldest months—October, November, and December. Due to the ground being frozen and the amount of bodies showing up daily, the mortuary had run out of room. They started to store the bodies in the underground tunnel system. When the tunnels became overcrowded, they then stored the remainder of the bodies in the basement of the YWCA until the ground thawed in the spring.

I do have a funny story I want to share, which happened in the nightclub. I went with my assistant Eric and we were both interviewing the tour guide about the hotel's history. My cell phone rang, and not wanting to interrupt our guide, I handed the phone to Eric. He talked for a minute, then said, "Mom, you might want to take this … it's NORAD." The look on our tour guide's face was priceless.

The two doorways to the tunnel. Each area is about ten feet deep and six feet wide. They are used for storage.

Both hallways dead end at a sealed-up doorway.

This building, which was built in 1902, prefers to stay anonymous. They were in the process of drywalling over the original tunnel entrances that lead underneath the sidewalks, and I was very lucky to be able to photograph them before they disappeared.

The building has many below ground vaults that extend underneath the sidewalks, which they have preserved and continue to use, along with the tunnel that my assistant, Eric, is seen standing in (next page).

One of the main problems with underground vaults is the risk of a vehicle or heavy machinery accidently driving up onto the sidewalk. The weight can collapse the vaults and cause a lot of damage. Because of this, the building's owner has installed a railing and seating areas on that part of the sidewalk. Hopefully, this will prevent anyone from driving over the vaults.

While it is disappointing that the tunnel entrances are being covered over, I am glad that the below ground vaults have been preserved.

Location Withheld
Colorado Springs

The inside of one of the large vaults under the sidewalk.

A blocked-off tunnel entrance ready for drywall.

A bricked-in doorway ready for drywall.

My assistant Eric standing in one of the many tunnels.

Lucky Devil Tattoo
20 East Bijou Street,
Colorado Springs

Skyline Nutrition
22 East Bijou Street,
Colorado Springs

This two-story commercial building was built in 1902 and originally housed a contractor and a tailor on the ground floor. The top floor housed the Caledonian Hall for over twenty years.

The Caledonian Society was founded in 1897 and its purpose and motto was "To promote friendly intercourse among persons of Scottish birth and descent in the City and Neighborhood and to keep alive and propagate a love for the music, literature, and ancient games of Scotland."

The front of this building has a large embedded crystal grate on the sidewalk in front of the entry doors. When I toured the basement, I discovered that this building had no tunnel entrance and no vault. The crystal grate simply helped to light up the basement area.

The end wall of the basement, which shows no connection to the tunnel system.

The crystal grate as seen from underneath.

This historic building has a unique crystal grate located at its entry door. Unlike the ones normally seen, this one has larger crystals. The metal threshold is also larger than most and is stamped "The Hassell Iron Works Co. Colorado Springs, Colo." The manager informed me that the grate simply lights up the basement and does not go to the street. I also asked him about the odd looking sidewalk outside his building. The metal-framed sections is what made me wonder about the existence of a possible tunnel or historic below ground entrance. Unfortunately, it is not historic. He explained that this odd looking sidewalk is simply a modern electrical switching station for the downtown area and is accessed through the two manhole covers.

Location withheld
Colorado Springs

The crystal grate outside the entry.

Framed-in sidewalk.

SEVENTEEN

The Broadmoor

Does The Broadmoor have tunnels?

Did they have a tunnel that led to a brothel?

Do they have a tunnel that leads to NORAD?

Are they storing an alien spacecraft under their lake?

Is there a tunnel that leads to Spencer Penrose's home?

Was there a tunnel from the old casino?

The land where The Broadmoor now sits was originally a farm owned by the Myers brothers. They purchased the land in the 1860s and grew corn that they used to make brooms. They sold their brooms in a shop in Old Colorado City.

In 1880, a man named William J. Willcox bought their farm and fifteen hundred acres of land on the mesa at the base of Cheyenne Mountain. He built a small dairy farm, which he named the Broadmoor Dairy.

In 1885, Willcox became partners with Count James Pourtales of Prussia, but by 1889 the dairy started to fail. (Prussia was a country from 1525 to 1947, which is now part of Germany, Poland, and the Soviet Union.)

The partners decided to use their land to build a town they called Broadmoor City. On July 1, 1891, they opened a European-style casino and in 1897, they opened a hotel located next door. Unfortunately, the casino burned down in 1897, but the hotel was saved. A smaller casino was built in 1898, but since it wasn't as grand as the first casino, it didn't prosper. In 1909, the buildings and the land were sold. The casino was used as a church and the hotel was used as a girl's school.

In May 1916, Spencer Penrose bought the property for $90,000 and announced that he was going to build "the finest hotel in the

United States." He made this decision in order to compete with the Antlers Hotel, which he was unable to purchase.

He had the casino moved and used it as his new golf clubhouse and re-named the original hotel the Colonial Club. The New Broadmoor opened June 1, 1918. The original hotel was torn down in 1961, and the casino was torn down in 1994.

When it comes to tunnels, The Broadmoor has four. These tunnels were built for the hotel staff to access the guest room buildings of Northlake, Northmoor, Southlake, and Southmoor. None of these tunnels left the hotel grounds. The tunnels are still in use and also hold all the utilities for the hotel. In the blueprint of the hotel's ground floor, one of the tunnels in the upper left hand corner is listed as "underground passage." It was quite common for the time period for hotel staff to use tunnels in order to not be seen by the guests.

As for a tunnel to a brothel, there wasn't one. The closest brothel was at the Cheyenne Canyon Inn, which was only about a mile away. There is no reason to build a mile-long tunnel, under a street, just to connect the hotel to a brothel.

There has also been a rumor that there is a secret tunnel from The Broadmoor to the North American Aerospace Defense Command (NORAD) for use by the president of the United States. There isn't. For this question, I contacted NORAD and received documents showing the history and construction of NORAD.

On page four of the Phase 1 construction manual, it mentions NORAD as having a large tunnel inside the mountain that is divided into three parts. The longest tunnel section is 2,630 feet long. They also built an access road that is thirty-eight feet wide from Highway 115, opposite Fort Carson and up Cheyenne Mountain, which took seventy-three days to construct. If the president was to visit, he is either driven up the road or flown to NORAD by helicopter. There is no reason to have a ten-mile-long underground tunnel to The Broadmoor … but he has stayed there.

The rumor that The Broadmoor is hiding an alien spacecraft for NORAD under their lake is the most original rumor that they have heard. The historian at NORAD joked that all the alien spacecrafts are stored at Area 51.

Is there a tunnel from The Broadmoor to the Spencer Penrose house? It's doubtful. The Penrose house is half a mile away down a residential street. I really doubt Mr. Penrose would have wanted to walk down a dark tunnel that was beneath the road his hotel guests drove on.

The question about the old casino having a tunnel doesn't make much sense after you learn the history of the building. The original casino burned down in 1897, and even if it did have a tunnel to the local brothel, it would have been a mile long.

I was told a funny story about The Broadmoor from the hotel's historian. As you can see in the ground floor blueprint, the hotel had an indoor pool. The pool was in use until 1963, when a floor was placed over it. That new floor now houses the hotel's shops. The interesting part is that the pool still looks the same underneath the floor and is used for storage. Slippery tile, rounded corners and steps still totally intact and ready for water.

The Broadmoor.
(Courtesy of The Broadmoor, Colorado Springs)

The original Broadmoor Hotel, built in 1897. (Courtesy Old Colorado City Historical Society)

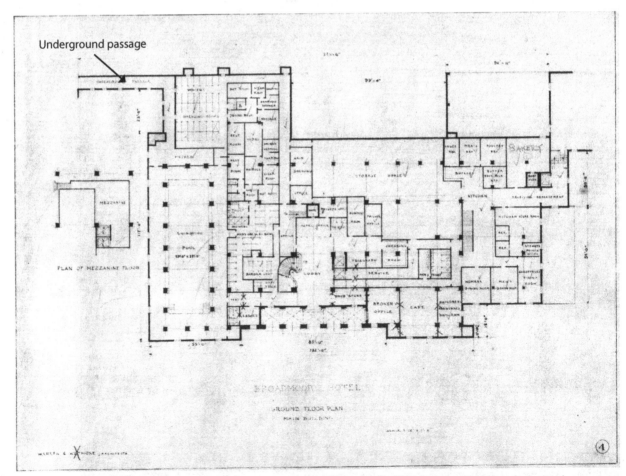

The original ground floor blueprint showing a tunnel and the pool. (Courtesy of The Broadmoor, Colorado Springs)

EIGHTEEN

Old Colorado City

Does the town really have tunnels?

Did the town really have a "wet side" and a "dry side"?

Were the tunnels used to hide from the police?

Who were "Thunder and Buttons"?

Old Colorado City has a history that dates back to 1859, when it was called El Dorado. The original settlement had around three hundred cabins and was renamed Colorado City in 1861. Unfortunately, the newly named town was failing. In 1863, Fountain Creek flooded and ruined the crops, which were then eaten by a plague of grasshoppers. To make matters worse, the town was constantly being raided by Civil War outlaws and the whole area had become unsafe.

As the town struggled to survive, General William Jackson Palmer was developing a town in 1871, just east of Colorado City, called Colorado Springs. Mr. Palmer established legislation that banned the sale of liquor within the city limits of his newly formed town. He stated that it would "promote a climate of strong moral standards." The residents of Colorado City decided to take advantage of this.

By the early 1900s, Colorado City was known as the rowdy, bawdy watering hole of Colorado Springs. They had illegal gambling, saloons, and a large red light district. The underground tunnels were used to allow people to go from the dry, reputable north side of the street to the wet and wild south side. The tunnels also allowed a quick way to exit the illegal gambling houses in case of a raid.

The town of Colorado City became known as " Old Town" to distinguish it from Colorado Springs, which was the "New Town." Colorado City later became known as Old Colorado City and eventually was made part of Colorado Springs in 1917.

Old Colorado City in 1884. (Courtesy Old Colorado City Historical Society)

As I was doing research, I found a fascinating story from the early 1900s. A hunter had killed a female elk and while he was dressing it, he saw her two babies standing off to the side watching him. He felt very guilty, so he caught the two babies, put them in his wagon, took them back to Denver, and sold them at an animal auction. They were bought by John O'Brien, a train conductor in Colorado Springs. He loved the little elk and trained them to pull a wagon.

Thunder and Buttons—
Thunder is on the left side,
Buttons on the right.
(Courtesy author's collection)

He soon had a side business. On his days off, he would hook the elk up to the wagon and run a taxi service from Old Colorado City to Colorado Springs. When it snowed, the elk pulled a sleigh. John O'Brien's nickname "Prairie dog" came from a little gimmick he had in his wagon. He caught a prairie dog and put him into a little wheel in the front of his wagon, which ran around and around. He told people that that was his extra power in case the elk got tired.

This building has five metal grates on the sidewalk and what appears to be a door to a service elevator. The grates and the elevator door have all been filled in with concrete, in what appears to be an attempt to prevent water leaks. During an interview with an employee of the museum, I was informed that the original tunnel wall had been removed to make the area in the basement larger. I found many examples of this in Denver. I was not allowed in the basement.

The Michael Garman Museum

2418 West Colorado Avenue, Colorado Springs

Two metal grates which would have allowed light and fresh air into the below ground windows.

An area that appears to be a service elevator door. A grate can be seen to the right.

The Templeton Building

2502 West Colorado Avenue, Colorado Springs

This building, which was built in 1891, was home to The Oxford Club. The building has an open tunnel and numerous windows and doors. In an early 1900s photo, it shows that the building had an outside entry door into the basement. The condition of this photo was very poor quality and I opted not to use it.

Two doorways that lead into the open tunnel.

The jacks helping to hold up the sidewalk inside the tunnel. No steel beams were used in the original construction.

A sealed-up doorway into the tunnels.

A doorway leading to an open tunnel full of garbage. This unfortunately is a common use for old tunnels and vaults.

The inside of the open tunnel. Garbage can be seen along with the original wooden sidewalk overhead.

A large open window with original frame intact, but the glass has been removed.

A sealed-up door. The bricks used to seal up the doorway can be seen on the sides of the plywood. This doorway led to the outside entrance.

This view from the sidewalk shows the original coal doors that were lifted up to dump coal into the basement.

NINETEEN

Cripple Creek

Does Cripple Creek have tunnels?

Does Cripple Creek have any below ground shops?

Did people use the tunnels to avoid the red light district?

Did people move the dead under the streets?

The Cripple Creek area was originally called Pisgah Park. Robert Miller Womack and his father bought a homestead from Levi Welty in 1876 and started their hunt for gold. For fifteen years they dug hundreds of holes all over the mountains, which earned Robert the name "Crazy Bob."

Finally, on October 20, 1890, Bob discovered gold in Poverty Gulch. This led to a gold rush and a population of fifty thousand people in the area by 1894. The area was renamed Cripple Creek. There are many stories surrounding the reason for the name. The two most popular reasons are that the area had a crooked stream that crippled a cow, or that a miner fell off a roof, hit a dog, broke the dog's leg … which broke the man's arm. Either way, the name stuck.

Between 1897 and 1917, gold production was never less than $10 million a year. By 1917, total gold production was almost $300 million. It was around this time that the mines started to dry up and people started to leave. By 1920, only five thousand people lived in the area and that number gradually dropped to only a few hundred. The town was listed as a ghost town. Finally in 1991, the town was allowed to bring in casino gambling and the town came back to life.

When it comes to tunnels, Cripple Creek has two types, walking tunnels and mining tunnels. Both are located under the streets, but most are now filled in. For example, the Colorado Grand Casino building at one time housed a mortuary in the basement. Across the street, the Johnny Nolon's Casino building was a hospital. I was informed that there was a tunnel under Bennett Avenue that allowed the hospital to move bodies to the mortuary. The tunnel in the basement of the hospital was covered over when a new concrete floor was put in and the tunnel under Bennett Avenue collapsed and was filled in. The old mortuary's tunnels were also sealed up when the Colorado Grand Casino turned the basement into a restaurant.

At the courthouse I was able to read the minutes from town meetings. An entry on April 1, 1894, mentions tunnels. "You shall well and securely timber all workings and excavations through or under said streets and alleys wherever necessary in order to ensure the absolute safety thereof." Another entry, posted on July 6, 1897, mentions "the cave-in of the street on South Second Street from unsecured timbers."

It is possible that the old original tunnel system was simply old mining tunnels that were abandoned after the gold was removed. Since the tunnels were already there, why not use them?

Cripple Creek in 1893. (Courtesy Colorado Historical Society, all rights reserved)

The hotel, which was originally called the Collins Hotel, was built in the 1890s. Located in the front of the hotel is a below ground shop entrance, which holds the hotel's theater, complete with a stage and a bar. The hotel has a second entrance, which is why this area looks unused.

The Imperial Hotel
123 North Third Street,
Cripple Creek

The outside of the hotel showing the below ground shop.

A close-up of the below ground shop entrance. A boarded-up window and a door can be seen. Against the back wall is an old poster display board that was used for hanging advertisements for the night's show.

Grand Opera House (Burned out foundation)

320-326 East Myers Avenue, Cripple Creek

The Grand Opera House was built in 1897, but burned down in 1907. The opera house wasn't rebuilt because there were other opera houses in town. The location of the opera house was also an embarrassment to the "decent" people in town because it was located in the red light district.

The location is also why the building had a tunnel entrance under the streets. The tunnel ran from Bennett Avenue to the opera house, which allowed parents to take their children to the opera without having to see any of the "wicked painted ladies." The tunnel entrance has two doorways that both lead into a wide walkway. I was told that the local kids play here and it's called "Crypt Town."

If you look at the front entrance of the opera house, you will see that the tunnel entrances match the design of the doorways. A lot of thought was put into the design of this tunnel entrance.

The Grand Opera House. (Courtesy Denver Public Library Western History Collection, #X-768)

The tunnel entrances as seen today.

The inside of the tunnel entrance with arched ceilings.

TWENTY

Leadville

Does Leadville have tunnels?

Does Leadville have any below ground shops?

In 1859, gold was first discovered in an area called California Gulch. By 1861, there were over six thousand prospectors swarming the area, which they named Oro City. The gold soon dried up and by the 1870s the area was deserted.

In 1877, Alvinius Woods and William Stevens discovered silver in the same area and the silver boom was born. The new town was named Leadville and it was incorporated in January 1878. The name was chosen because the local sand was composed of lead with an extremely high silver content.

By 1880, the town of forty thousand residents had over a dozen smelters and was covered in a blanket of noxious black and yellow smoke. It is said that people could predict the weather by the way the smoke from the smokestacks was behaving. If it rose high and straight, the weather was going to be good. If the smoke slid back down the outside of the stacks and over the rooftops of cabins, a storm was on the way.

In the early 1900s, molybdenum was discovered in Climax, which is fourteen miles northeast of Leadville. This metal is used in the production of high-strength steel alloys. By the 1940s, the Climax Mine was producing over $13 million a year.

Leadville, also called "Cloud City," is located at an elevation of 10,200 feet. This makes it the highest city in the country.

When it comes to tunnels and below ground shops, I heard a lot of stories but only found the remains of two.

Historic Leadville. (Courtesy Pueblo City-County Library District, Western History Collection)

This building is an historic, two-story brick building. Inside the basement I was able to see a tunnel entrance and two windows with original glass. The large tunnel entrance had been covered over with plywood and a coal chute installed. This doorway appears large enough for a double door. The basement area was around five hundred and sixty square feet and may have been a small shop or a storage room.

Empty Building
316 Harrison Avenue, Leadville

The tunnel entrance with a coal chute.

One of two windows, which are located in the back of the building, and would have had grates.

Quincy's Steak and Spirits

416 Harrison Avenue, Leadville

This resturant is located in the Quincy building, which was built in 1879. In the basement of the building is a wonderful below ground grocery store. It has a wooden door and open areas for more doors and large windows, which unfortunately are no longer there. The store was originally accessed from the sidewalk by a staircase that led into the underground tunnel system. The original rocks on the walls of the tunnel have been smoothed over with concrete. As you walk down the tunnel, you can see a manhole cover and a grate above your head.

There is also another historic feature located within the Quincy building, but next door in 422 Harrison. When the floors were being restored, a historic cistern was discovered beneath them. In order to keep this unique piece of the building's history, the cistern was cleaned up and covered over with a large piece of plexiglass. The owners have lit it up with lights and have placed all the old bottles they found inside of it around the rim.

It would be wonderful if the historic below ground grocery store was also cleaned up and people were allowed to visit the last of the Leadville tunnels.

The cistern located next door in the resturant at 422 Harrison.

The original wooden door.

The large openings that could be for a door or a large window.

The inside of the tunnel. The original rocks have been covered with concrete. The sidewalk is overhead.

TWENTY-ONE

Fort Collins

Does Fort Collins have tunnels?

Were the tunnels used to herd cattle during the winter?

Were the tunnels used to transport prisoners?

Was Disneyland's Main Street based on Fort Collins?

The history of Fort Collins does not start with the name of a town, but with the name of a stage stop. In 1862, soldiers were sent from the Ninth Kansas Cavalry at Fort Laramie to protect the Cherokee Trail and the Overland Stage line.

General James Craig decided that the stage stop needed a proper name so he named it Camp Collins after William O. Collins, the commander of the Ohio Cavalry stationed at Fort Laramie. Soon after, the Kansas Cavalry was replaced by Colorado troops.

In May 1864, Commander Collins returned with his troops to relieve the Colorado soldiers, but on the night of June 9, 1864, a flood rushed down the canyon and destroyed Camp Collins. On August 20, 1864, Commander Collins signed an order choosing their new location, and in October 1864, the new camp was ready. It was also decided to re-name the new camp Fort Collins despite the fact that the camp was not a fort—it didn't have any walls.

The fort was closed down in September 1866, and the soldiers were relieved of their duty. Some soldiers loved the area and decided to stay. The town of Fort Collins was incorporated on February 3, 1873.

Fort Collins voted to make the town a "dry town," but also voted to allow "sample rooms" in 1884. A sample room was not a saloon, but a room in the back of a store where alcohol could be purchased in a quiet, calm environment. Since alcohol was still illegal, the sample rooms would pay a fine in order to remain open. In 1895, it was voted to close all the sample rooms and the town went totally dry until 1969. Ironically, Fort Collins is now the second largest producer of beer in the state of Colorado.

When anyone in Fort Collins thinks of tunnels, they think of the Colorado State University campus. This type of tunnel is not what I researched and I feel any information I give on this type of tunnel would just cause problems for the college. I have heard that these tunnels are used for steam heat from the local steam plant and the pipes could easily burn or kill someone.

The stories of using the historic tunnels to transport cattle I find quite comical. I have read stories about how the lack of shelter and the cold winters might have forced ranchers to move their cattle underground. As a Colorado native, I have seen many cows standing in fields during a snowstorm, all huddled together to keep warm. I have also watched ranchers struggle to load cattle into trucks. I could not imagine herding cattle into a dark, cold, musty tunnel that is only four or five feet wide just to transport them across town. And I don't think the store owners above would appreciate the smell or the mess.

Downtown Fort Collins in the 1940s. (Courtesy Denver Public Library Western History Collection, #X-11009)

I did find an 1882 newspaper article that mentioned below ground shops under the opera house. They housed a dressmaker, a toy shop, and one of Fort Collins' famous sample rooms. They advertised "Prohibition drinks of all kinds which regulate the solar system and steady the nerves."

Now when it comes to Walt Disney using Old Town as his inspiration for Main Street at Disneyland … that's all true. A Fort Collins native named Harper Goff, who was born in 1911, worked for Walt Disney and showed him pictures of his hometown. In turn, Disney showed him pictures of his hometown of Marceline, Missouri. Together they combined the towns' structures and used the building designs on Disneyland's Main Street.

Outside this store I discovered below ground shops covered over by a large grate. Small concrete bridges allow customers to enter the shops on the street level. On one end I found a gate and the staircase used to enter the below ground shops. These areas are very similar to the below ground shops that I found in Trinidad.

The owner told me that the basement is still broken into rooms or shop areas and that the original doors and windows have either been drywalled over or boarded up. I was not allowed into the basement to take pictures.

Sole Mates
172 North College Avenue, Fort Collins

The gate used to enter the staircase to the below ground shops.

The large grates covering the below ground shop areas. Looking through the grates you can see the original doors and windows of the shops.

Location Withheld
Old Town, Fort Collins

I discovered this old below ground shop while walking around Old Town. As you can see, on the back wall is a sealed-up doorway that would have led underneath the sidewalk.

A below ground shop with a sealed-up doorway that led under the sidewalk.

The sealed-up tunnel entrance used to transport prisoners to the Silver Grill for meals.

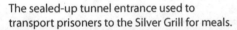

Happy Lucky's Tea House and Treasures
236 Walnut Street,
Fort Collins

Silver Grill
218 Walnut Street
(originally 212 Walnut Street), Fort Collins

Happy Lucky's Tea House and Treasures is located inside the historic firehouse. The basement of this building originally held the town's jail. The story goes that twice a day the prisoners were chained together and walked through a tunnel into the basement of what is now the Silver Grill, one hundred and fifty feet away. One day the jailer transported six prisoners to the Silver Grill for their meal, but when they arrived back to the jail … there were only five. The sixth man was never found.

This amazing coffee shop, which is named after the Van Gogh painting, has a wonderful partial tunnel in their basement. The tunnel has been broken into two storage rooms and is sealed off at both ends. The rooms are both seven feet high and around nine feet deep. The original crystal-filled grates are still intact and wonderfully lit up by large florescent lights to attract customers to the coffee shop. Very clever.

Starry Night
112 South College Avenue, Suite 100, Fort Collins

The inside of the storage room showing the width of the original tunnel.

The tunnels, now sealed up and turned into storage rooms.

The crystal-filled grate from inside the tunnel.

The crystal-filled grate from outside the coffee shop.

Bondi Beach Bar and Grill

11 Old Town Square #120,
Fort Collins

CoCo Artist Studio

11 Old Town Square #121A,
Fort Collins

Little Bird

11 Old Town Square #121,
Fort Collins

These three businesses are in the F. Miller block, built in 1888. In front of the building are seven crystal-filled metal grates. These grates are not letting in light for a historic tunnel, but rather for window wells. I was not allowed into the basements, so I don't know if the windows are exposed or covered up.

On the outside wall of the Little Bird business is a wonderful below ground shop entrance. It does not appear that the shop was part of the tunnel system, as the stones on the back wall match the original stones against the building. Also, there are three more window wells with crystal-filled metal grates right past the below ground shop entrance. The windows would not have window wells inside of a tunnel.

The below ground shop entrance.

One of ten crystal-filled grates.

This store, which sells sporting goods, also has a wonderful below ground shop located right outside its front door. This shop has one sealed-up window and two doors. The employee I spoke with told me how the below ground shop connects to the tunnel system, but is blocked by a blue wooden door. He also mentioned how the employees hate to go into the basement because it's really, really creepy. Because of this, the employee wouldn't take me downstairs to take pictures.

The Wright Life
200 Linden Street,
Fort Collins

The outside entrance to the below ground shop.

Witton block

Location Withheld,
Fort Collins

The Witton block was built in 1905. John Witton was an Irishman and his store sold clothing, furnishings, boots, and shoes. Both buildings share a basement space. Located in the shared basement are two sealed-up doorways. After speaking to the owner, he did confirm that the doorways led into the tunnel system, which joined with another tunnel system across the street.

The first sealed-up doorway.

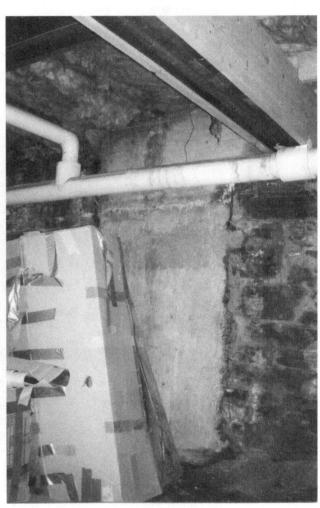

The second sealed-up doorway.

TWENTY-TWO
Watching History Being Destroyed

May 20, 2014, was a dark day in Pueblo, Colorado. I drove past The Great Divide bike shop to see that their beautiful, historic tunnel was being destroyed. All three vault rooms were exposed to the daylight and twenty feet of the tunnel system was torn open.

I went inside the bike shop to find a very upset store owner. He explained that the Pueblo Planning and Community Development Department was destroying history in an attempt to keep large delivery trucks from turning onto Santa Fe Avenue. When he showed them the tunnel system and the carefully preserved vaults, they told him that they were not "historically significant." A store owner does not own the areas under the sidewalk, so the bike shop's owner had no way to fight the destruction.

Labeled the "4th Street Signalization Project," the owner of the bike shop was sent an email of the proposed concrete planters that would now replace his century-old vaults and twenty feet of his ninety-six-foot long tunnel.

On 4th Street, which houses the tunnel, the planter will be approximately eighteen feet long by seventeen feet deep. For this, the city removed twenty feet of his tunnel. On the Santa Fe side, which housed the vaults, the planters will be approximately thirty-six feet long and twenty-four feet deep. For this they removed all three vaults, which equaled forty-three feet seven inches. On the edge of the destruction, I could see the roof of the below ground vault next door at Racine's Locksmithing & Security. Luckily, they didn't continue their destruction down the block.

The twenty feet that was removed from the tunnel. By doing this, the tunnel also lost a window. The steel supports can be seen that used to hold up the arched ceiling.

The current view from inside the tunnel. The plywood wall will soon become a concrete block wall.

All three vault rooms, with the partition walls removed, ready to be filled in with dirt.

One of the vault rooms, opened up and ready to be filled in with dirt.

This is the door that used to lead to the historic vaults. Soon, the plywood will be replaced with a concrete block wall.

Example of the concrete planters that will be installed.

Bibliography

Ackroyd, Peter. *London Under.* Doubleday Books, 2011.

Armstrong, Helen. *The Walking Tour: A Guide to Old Colorado City.* Text Pros, Manitu Springs, 2000.

Bertozzi-Villa, Elena. *Broadmoor Memories: The History of the Broadmoor.* Pictorial Histories Publishing Company Inc., 1993.

"Bill Speidel's Underground Tour." Interview and Tourist advertisement, Seattle, Washington.

Bishop, Mary Harelkin. *Tunnels of Time.* Coteau Books, 2000.

Blair, Edward. *Leadville: Colorado's Magic City.* Pruett Publishing, 1980.

Bryan, Ray. *Four Historic Walking Tours of Pueblo, Colorado.* Pueblo County Historical Society, 1983.

Debusk, Honora. *Early Life in Trinidad and Purgatory Valley.* Colorado College, 1930.

Dinar, Joshua. *Denver Then and Now.* Thunder Bay Press, 2002.

"Ellinwood's Underground World." Interview and Tourist advertisement, Ellinwood, Kansas.

Finley, Judith Reid. *Time Capsule 1900: Colorado Springs a Century Ago.* Pastwords Publications, 1998.

Forrest, Kenton, and Charles Albi. *Denver's Railroads.* Colorado Railroad Museum, 1981.

Fry, Eleanor. *Salida: The Early Years.* Arkansas Valley Publishing Co., 2001.

"Havre Beneath the Streets." Interview and Tourist advertisement, Havre, Montana.

"Jacksonville Top to Bottom Walking Tour." Interview and Tourist advertisement, Jacksonville, Florida.

Levine, Brian H. *Cities of Gold: Victor, Cripple Creek Mining District.* Century One Press, 1981.

Morris, Steve. *Boomtown: A Brief History of Florence and Surrounding Areas.* Fremont Middle School Local History Class, 1981.

"NORAD Combat Operations Center, Phase 1 Construction." Utah Construction and Mining Co., San Francisco, California.

"NORAD's Underground COC." Unclassified, 1956–1966.

Patent: Forming Glass Into Conical Figures and Lamps, number 372, 1704.

Patent: Glasses and Lamps for Ships, Mines, etc., number 232, 1684.

Patent: Improvement of Pavement Lights, number 2014, July 31, 1871.

Patent: Improvement of Vault Lights, number 123,688, February 13, 1872.

Patent: Vault Cover, number 10,921, April 10, 1888.

Patent: Vault Cover, number 4,266, November 12, 1845.

"Pendleton Underground." Interview and Tourist advertisement. Pendleton, Oregon.

"Portland Walking Tours." Interview and Tourist advertisement, Portland, Oregon.

"Repair and Rehabilitation of Historic Sidewalk Vault Lights." Preservation Tech Notes, National Park Service, U.S. Department of the Interior, New York, New York.

Seanson, Evedene Burris. *Fort Collins Yesterday.* Don-Art Printers Inc., 1975.

Smith, Duane A. *Rocky Mountain Boom Town: A History of Durango, Colorado.* University Press of Colorado, 1992.

Taylor, Donna. *Memories From the Foot of the Gorge.* Cañon City High School Printing Class, 1969.

"The Blake Street Vault." Interview and Tourist advertisement, Denver, Colorado.

The British Architect: A Journal of Architecture and Accessory Arts. Volume 32, January 1890.

"The Eureka Springs Downtown Underground Tour." Interview and Tourist advertisement, Eureka Springs, Arkansas.

"The Fort Collins Ghost Tour." Interview and Tourist advertisement, Fort Collins, Colorado.

"The Stanley Hotel." Interview and Tourist advertisement, Estes Park, Colorado.

"The Ultimate Underground Tour." Interview and Tourist advertisement, Cincinnati, Ohio.

"The Underground Tour." Interview and Tourist advertisement, Sacramento, California.

"Underground Atlanta." Interview and Tourist advertisement, Atlanta, Georgia.

"Use of Space Beneath Sidewalks." Article VIII adopted March 27, 1923, by the Borough of Pen Argyl, Pennsylvania.

Index

Atlanta, Georgia, underground tours, 20
Auraria, 53

Babylonia, vaults in, 1, 2
Blake Street Vault tours, 19
Broadmoor, The
    History of, 139–142

Caledonian Society, The, 136
Camp Collins, 159
Cañon City
    Anita McCoy Dance Studio, 106
    Bresnan Communications, 105
    Haley's Cañon Western Wear, 104
    History of, 99–103
    Holy Cross Abbey, 103
    McClure-Strathmore Hotel, 108
    Vault light cover in, 4, 5
Capone, Al, 125–126
Churches with underground vaults, 2
Cincinnati, Ohio, underground tours, 20
Colorado Fuel and Iron Company, Pueblo, 29
Colorado Springs
    History of, 131–132
    Lucky Devil Tattoo, 136
    Skyline Nutrition, 136
    Underground Bar, 133
Colorado State Mental Hospital, Pueblo, 28
Colorado State Militia, 45
Cripple Creek
    Gold rush, 149
    Grand Opera House, 152
    History of, 149–150
    Imperial Hotel, 151
Cross vault, 1

Deck light, 3
Dempsey, Jack, 85, 94
Denver & Rio Grande Railroad, 70, 82–83, 111
Denver
    Anti-Chinese movement, 54
    Barclay Hotel, 66
    Barth Hotel, 66
    Connected hotels 62
    EVOO Marketplace, 61
    History of, 53–55
    Mattie's House of Mirrors, 56–57
    Oxford Hotel, 67
    Prostitutes, 55
    Rio Grande Mexican Restaurant, 58
    The Blake Street Vault, 58
    Tramway Power House, 65
    Union Station, 62–67
    Windsor Hotel, 65
    Windsor Stables, 66

Denver, James W., 54
Denver's Railroads, 62, 63
Destroying hollow sidewalks, 10, 11
Destroying underground vaults, 10
Double-barreled vault, 1
"Double cupboard," 2
Durango
    Animas Trading Company, 77
    Below Ground Shop Entrances 73
    Hangings, 72
    History of, 70–73
    May Palace, 80
    The Steaming Bean, 78
    Vault light cover in, 3, 4
Dust orbs, 14

Egypt, vaults in, 1
Ellinwood, Kansas
    Preserving hollow sidewalks, 11, 13
    Underground tours, 19
    Vault light cover in, 3, 6
Eureka Springs, Arkansas, underground tours, 21
Evens, Laura, 55

Florence
    Cañon National Bank, 121
    Florence Flower Shop, 118
    Florence Pioneer Museum, 115
    Good Stuff Antiques, 121
    History of, 111–112
    Hotel Florence, 119
    Lovell Block, 120
    McCandless Building, 116
    Smokestack, 114
Florence and Cripple Creek Railroad, 112
Flu pandemic of 1918, 134
Fort Collins
    Bondi Beach Bar and Grill, 164
    CoCo Artist Studio, 164
    Happy Lucky's Tea House and Treasures, 162
    History of, 159–161
    Little Bird, 164
    Silver Grill, 162
    Sole Mates, 161
    Starry Night, 163
    Witton block, 166
    Wright Life, 165

Ghost orbs, 15–16, 17
Ghosts, 16–17
Gin recipe, 26
Graveyards with underground vaults, 2
Gravity and Bronco Street Railroad, 56
Great Seattle Fire, 24
Groin vault, 1

Havre, Montana, underground tours, 21
Hollow sidewalks, 8, 10
Hyatt, Thaddeus, 3

Jacksonville, Florida, underground tours, 22

King, Steven, 51
Knights of Pythias, 118
Kroenig, William, 99
Ku Klux Klan, 100–101, 102, 103

Larimer, William H., Jr., 53, 54
Leadville
    History of, 154–155
      Quincy's Steak and Spirits, 156
      Vault light cover in, 4
Lighting below-ground vaults, 7
Ludlow Massacre, 29, 112

McCandless, James A., 111, 112

"Negro" parlor, 71
New York City, vault lights in, 3
North American Aerospace Defense Command
    (NORAD), 140

Old Colorado City
    History of, 143–144
      Michael Garman Museum, 145
      Templeton Building, 146
      Thunder and Buttons, 144
Orbs, 14–15

Palmer, William Jackson, 131, 132, 143
Pendleton, Oregon, underground tours, 23
Penrose, Spencer, 139–140
Pike, Zebulon, 99
Portland, Oregon, underground tours, 23
Preserving underground vaults, 10, 11
Prohibition, 21, 23, 45, 54, 67, 161
Prostitutes, 55, 56, 72, 84, 116, 152
Pueblo
    Colorado Fuel and Iron Company, 29
    Colorado State Mental Hospital, 28
    Flood of 1921, 26–27
    Golden M Southwestern and Indian Art, 34
    History of, 25
    Johnco's Used Furniture, 38
    Olde Time Antiques, 31
    Pinelle's Bowlero Lanes, 30
    Racine's Locksmithing & Security, 39
    Smelters, 25
    The Edge—Ski, Paddle, and Pack, 37
    The Great Divide Ski, Bike and Hike, 40
    Town's first gin mill, 26
    Union Antiques, 36
Pueblo's 4th Street Signalization Project, 167

Raton Pass, 124
Rockwell, Edward, 3

Rogers, Jennie, 56
Roman Empire, vaults in, 1–2
Roosevelt, Theodore, 100
Royal Gorge War, The, 82

Sacramento, California, underground tours, 21
Salida
    Beadsong, 92
    Culture Clash, 87
    Fat Tees, 92
    First Colorado Land Office, 90
    Handlebars Barbershop, 93
    History of, 82–85
    Mixing Bowl, 86
    Monarch Brokers, 93
    Mountain Vista Properties, 92
    Pinon Real Estate Group, 96
    Royal Gorge War, 82
    Seasons Celebrations, 92
    Strait-McKenna Buildings, 85
    Sunshine Market, 93
    Unique Theater, 91
Santa Fe Trail, 124
Seattle, Washington, underground tours, 24
Silks, Mattie, 56, 57
Speakeasys, 45, 47
Stanley Hotel, The
    Construction of, 51
    Electricity in, 51
    History of, 50–51
    Tours, 18
Stanley, Freeland Oscar, 50

The Shining, 51
Thunder and Buttons, 144
Trinidad
    History of, 124–126
    Main Street, 127–129
    Mission at the Bell, 130

Ute Indians, 100
Union Station, Denver, 62–67

Vault light covers, 3–6
Vault light panels, 5, 61, 107, 109, 137, 138, 163, 164
Vault lights, 3–6
Vaults, oldest, 1
Victor
    Burning of, 112, 113
    City Hall, 49
    History of, 41–42
    Kinnikinnik Emporium, 44
    Monarch Saloon, 48
    The Claim Jumper, 42
    Vault light cover in, 4
    Victor Elks Lodge, 45

Water damage to below ground vaults, 8
Westinghouse Mazda Lamps Lighting Service, 106
Womack, Robert Miller, 149
Wyndus, Edward, 3